T0277392

A GUIDE TO MAKING LEATHER
BELTS
WITH 12 COMPLETE PROJECTS

A GUIDE TO MAKING LEATHER
BELTS
WITH 12 COMPLETE PROJECTS

NIGEL ARMITAGE

SCHIFFER
PUBLISHING
4880 Lower Valley Road • Atglen, PA 19310

Other Schiffer Books by the Author
Leathercraft, Nigel Armitage,
ISBN 978-0-7643-6039-8

Other Schiffer Books on Related Subjects
Practical Leatherwork, Carsten Bothe,
ISBN 978-0-7643-5744-2
Quilted Leather, Cathy Wiggins,
ISBN 978-0-7643-5500-4
Little Delights in Leather, Mélanie Voituriez,
ISBN 978-0-7643-5838-8

© 2022 Design and layout, BlueRed Press
© 2022 Text and images, Nigel Armitage

Photography on the following pages by Jason Elberts of Jet
Productions: Back cover, 2, 6, 14, 157, 160

Library of Congress Control Number: 2021952658

All rights reserved. No part of this work may be reproduced
or used in any form or by any means—graphic, electronic, or
mechanical, including photocopying or information storage
and retrieval systems—without written permission from the
publisher.

The scanning, uploading, and distribution of this book or any
part thereof via the internet or any other means without the
permission of the publisher is illegal and punishable by law.
Please purchase only authorized editions and do not
participate in or encourage the electronic piracy of
copyrighted materials.

"Schiffer," "Schiffer Publishing, Ltd.," and the pen and inkwell
logo are registered trademarks of Schiffer Publishing, Ltd.

Produced by BlueRed Press Ltd. 2021
Designed by Insight Design
Type set in Berling

ISBN: 978-0-7643-6427-3
Printed in India

Published by Schiffer Publishing, Ltd.
4880 Lower Valley Road
Atglen, PA 19310
Phone: (610) 593-1777; Fax: (610) 593-2002
Email: Info@schifferbooks.com
Web: www.schifferbooks.com

For our complete selection of fine books on this and related
subjects, please visit our website at www.schifferbooks.com.
You may also write for a free catalog.

Schiffer Publishing's titles are available at special discounts
for bulk purchases for sales promotions or premiums.
Special editions, including personalized covers, corporate
imprints, and excerpts, can be created in large quantities
for special needs. For more information, contact the publisher.

We are always looking for people to write books on new
and related subjects. If you have an idea for a book, please
contact us at proposals@schifferbooks.com.,

Schiffer Publishing's titles are available at special discounts
for bulk purchases for sales promotions or premiums. Special
editions, including personalized covers, corporate imprints, and
excerpts, can be created in large quantities for special needs.
For more information, contact the publisher.

CONTENTS

Beginner   Intermediate   Advanced

INTRODUCTION

First, thank you—thank you for buying my book. Whether you are just finding your feet or are already an adept and seasoned leatherworker, I hope you will find something useful inside.

If you have my first book, then this is an excellent add-on. If you don't, it is a credible stand-alone, but buy the first one anyway—I've a washing machine to pay off!

This book is entirely about making belts. A lot of what is said is repeated, but I make no apologies for that. Were you to work from the first to last in one go, it might feel repetitive; however, it will just serve as reinforcement, and that is no bad thing.

This is not a book on how to do leatherwork; it's about how to make belts. Belts are underrated, or at least the idea of how much work it takes to make one is. A great many belts being made today aren't as good as they could/should be. Many people mistakenly believe making a belt is a simple and easy thing—and, believing them to be easy, some people don't prepare in the right way to make an item of high quality.

A good belt is invaluable, so it's unsurprising that time, effort, and planning are needed to make one. If you take only one thing from this book, it is that.

The belts I have chosen to make and explain each have a reason: there are ones to cover a broad range of abilities, some have historic value, and some a specific purpose.

It is fair to say that the belt is one of the oldest and most often-made leather items, yet it is frequently underrated and undervalued. I hope that together we can do it more justice.

Enjoy!
Nigel

AN APOLOGY

I am left-handed, and for as long as I have been using rulers to measure, I have been using them upside down. After all these years, an upside down ruler looks as normal to me as a ruler the right way up.

As such, when making the belts, I set them to suit me, left-handed, and all the rulers are upside down. I wouldn't have noticed but for looking at the photographs!

I can see that this could be irritating, and I apologize. If nothing else, it is a quirky insight into the world of a left-hander and to be fair . . . no southpaw would even notice.

ANATOMY OF A BELT

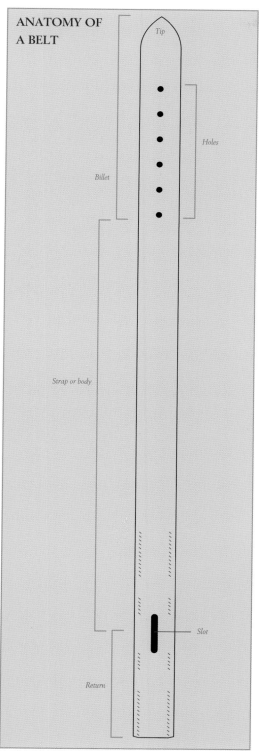

Tip

Holes

Billet

Strap or body

Slot

Return

The measurements used in this book are in metric, which is a clear unit and will help you with precision. If you are able to work in metric, it will make things easier.

However, if you are more used to working with imperial easurements, these two charts can assist you with any conversions you may need.

mm	Oz.
0.4	1
0.8	2
1.2	3
1.6	4
2	5
2.4	6
2.8	7
3.2	8
3.6	9
4	10
4.4	11
4.8	12

mm	Inches
1	0.039
2	0.079
3	0.118
4	0.158
5	0.197
6	0.236
7	0.276
8	0.315
9	0.354
10	0.394
11	0.433
12	0.472
13	0.512
14	0.551
15	0.591
16	0.630
17	0.669
18	0.709
19	0.748
20	0.787
30	1.181
40	1.575
50	1.969
60	2.362
70	2.756
80	3.150
90	3.543
100	3.937

ANATOMY OF A BUCKLE

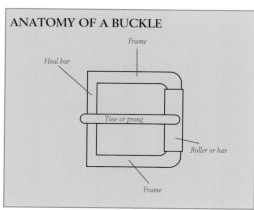

Frame

Heal bar

Tine or prong

Roller or bar

Frame

TOOLS

As with many areas of leatherwork, specialist tools can be called on to do certain jobs. Belt making is no exception—the phrase, "the right tool for the job," comes to mind here. In the skills section of this book I will look at the use of some of these specialist tools, along with how to do the job by using other techniques and what you may already have available.

Having the right tool will benefit you hugely. This is a list of tools I recommend you have to be able to make quality belts. Where to buy these tools is listed at the back of the book.

1. Beveler/edger: This little tool is designed to take a fine bevel off the leather at the edge. It is the perfect tool to help dress edges and protect them from damage.

2. Crease: This tool has two jobs. It adds a level of detail to plain leather edges and also prevents moisture from seeping in from the edge, so preventing water stains.

3. Crew punch: Also called a bag or oblong punch. This is for adding the slit to a strip of leather where a buckle will sit, to allow the prong to pass through.

4. Cutting edge: A much heavier tool than a ruler and rarely marked with any measurements, it is purely a guide for cutting. Two inches (50 mm) wide, thick, and heavy is best.

5. Cutting mat: While there are many boards available, a self-healing cutting mat is great, because it is inexpensive and widely available.

6. Disks: An excellent and cheaper alternative to a strap end punch and a great tool to help with fancy stitching.

7. Dividers: Also called wing dividers or a scratch compass and the perfect tool for tracing a fine line along the edge of leather that dictates the distance from the edge to where your stitching needs to be.

8. French skive: A very thin and sharp-angled knife for taking thin layers of leather off. It's used to thin strap ends or take edges off.

9. Hammer/maul: These are mainly used to strike irons and punches. Such tools are made of steel—so your hammer cannot be—steel on steel will damage your tools. Nylon or polymer is recommended; wood is too slick and can be damaged, and rubber will bounce. You are looking for a hammer (or maul) that will give a dead blow with no bounce that can cause a second strike—it's very frustrating if the tool moves between strikes.

10. Hole punch: Single and rotary options. The ideal tool to make round holes for belts, rivets, studs, and the like.

11. Irons: Designed to mark the holes where you want to stitch, traditionally these would be pricking irons used together with an awl to make the holes for each stitch. This takes much time and practice. At the start, I recommend you use one of the new stitching irons. These fully make the holes, allowing you to stitch without spending many hours learning how to use an awl. An awl will be needed at a later stage, but let's get you started first.

12. Knives: There are just too many to recommend one above the others, so I will list the qualities you need to look for in a knife. Above all, good steel—you will spend less time keeping it sharp. It should be thin but not flexible; you don't want the blade to vary under pressure. Plus a good, comfortable handle.

13. Needles: Saddlers' harness needles with blunt points are designed for stitching leather and are available in a variety of sizes.

14. Pulling block: With the new irons acting like a row of awl blades, we need to ensure the iron comes out perfectly straight, the same way as it went in. To help with this, use a small wooden block to keep the leather flat while pulling the iron out.

15. Ruler: A steel ruler is an invaluable tool for measuring and cutting against. Precision is important, so get a good one; also, a few different lengths will prove helpful.

16. Ruler stop: An excellent tool to ensure consistent measuring. A must-have tool!

17. Scratch Awl: Also called a clickers awl. This small tool is basically a fine spike in a handle. It is the perfect tool for marking and drawing on leather.

18. Slicker: A lovely little tool that, when used with moisture or an edge compound, slicks the edges of the leather down to a fine sheen. Canvas is also a firm favorite with some.

19. Snips/scissors: A must for snipping thread, since this needs to be done with a level of accuracy. They must be sharp.

20. Strap end punch: The perfect tool to put an English or round point on a strap for making belts, bags, and watch straps.

21. Thread: There are many variants of thread suitable for stitching leather; some of the best are linen, nylon, and polyester.

19
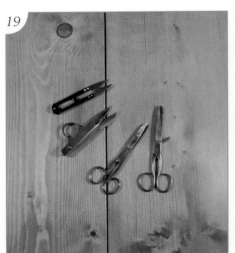

20

21

22. Saddlers clam: This is a very important piece of equipment designed to hold an item steady to allow you to saddle-stitch.

23. Sanding tools: Any sandpaper will work for roughing up or sanding edges, but there are a few inexpensive tools that will help with these tasks, such as sanding blocks and sanding sticks. They are not specific to leatherwork and are widely available at most hardware stores or online.

24. Setting hammer: A good dome-headed hammer or smasher will flatten your stitching or assist with the bonding of a glued edge.

25. Square: Any good-quality square that will give you an accurate right angle will do the job.

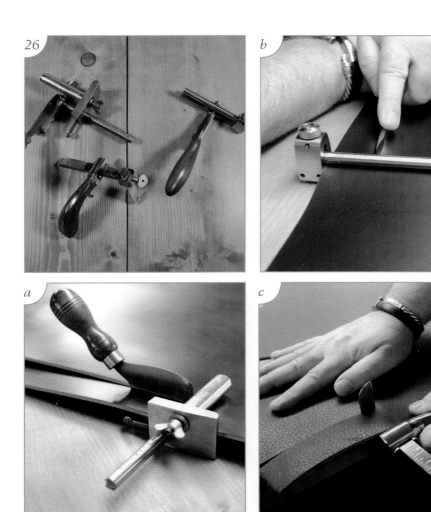

26. Strap cutter: Strap cutters are an invaluable tool for cutting straps and strips of leather evenly.

They are commonly found in two styles: plough gauges (on the left and right in photo 26 and in photos *a* and *b*), which are used by pushing away, and draw gauges (in the center in photo 26 and in photo *c*), by pulling toward you.

MATERIALS AND HARDWARE

LEATHER

I have no doubt you appreciate what a very broad subject choosing the right leather can be, and location will play a huge part in this. Being located in the UK, I favor leathers I can source locally, and I am fortunate to have such sources available as Sedgwick & Co., Metropolitan Leather, and J. & F. J. Bakers & Co. All have been established for well over a hundred years.

The belts in this book are expected to do a job, do that job well, and last a long time.

In view of this, the leather needs to be strong, not to fold over when tension is applied by the belt loops, and not to stretch when worn normally or when wet.

While I will be using leathers from the above suppliers to make the following projects, it may not be that helpful to you if you are located far from the UK, although they do all ship internationally. To try to assist with this, I am going to talk about the type of leather that makes a good belt, why it is a good choice, and what to look for.

BRIDLE BUTT
This is usually found up to 4–6 mm thick. It is stuffed full of waxes and oils when it's being made, making it dense, firm, and less prone to stretch. It is not disposed to distortion and is ideal for items designed for outdoor use. But it is much harder to work—and especially stitch—although the benefits far outweigh the difficulties you may face.

SHOULDER
This leather is much easier to work, is easier to finish, and looks very nice with little effort. It is a softer leather than bridle but is more prone to stretching under tension, especially if it gets wet. It is ideal for a fashion belt that is going to be worn loose. It is also a good choice to face belts with, since the color options are much broader. Indeed, this is what I use to face the Raised Belt (p.101), and to line the Lined Belt (p. 91).

SIDE
This is not the best cut for straps, although this depends on the tanning process. If you are using side, it is the top edge you want to be working from, as this is the thickest and strongest part.

In short, any leather can be used as you can do things to strengthen it, but it is just far better to use the right leather for the job in the first place. The tanning process evidently plays a big part as well as the cut, so getting the combination right will go a long way to ensure quality.

BUCKLES

All buckles are not equal!

We can spend a lot of money on our leather and invest a lot of time in making our belts, only to find the buckle lets us down.

Look at what the belt does and is expected to do, and what the purpose of the buckle is. Most of the time, there is no great strain on a buckle. If a belt is being worn as a fashion accessory, it will rarely if ever be put to the test. It is when we come to rely on the belt to do a proper job other than keep our pants up—such as carrying a knife sheath—that this can change.

Using a buckle that looks nice but is made of a cast alloy cannot be relied on not to break.

Choose one with a tine that is too thin, and it can bend.

These are extreme requests of a buckle, I appreciate, but if you are using the best leather you can get . . . would it not be fair so say the same of the buckle?

I tend to use solid brass or steel, hardware that I can rely on to make belts my customers can rely on. After all, who knows what else they could be used for. Using the right materials means you are making it right—and if you make it right, you need to make it only once!

I make mention a lot in this book about measuring points: the critical points used to measure the length of the belt. The placement of the measuring point on the buckle template is dictated by the distance from the heel bar to the tine or prong where it meets the frame.

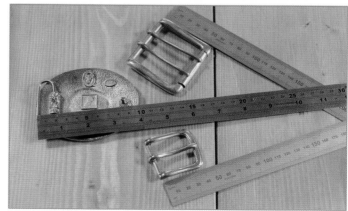

RIVETS

I am not enthusiastic about rivets. Most items I make tend to be stitched. There are occasions, however, where rivets are useful, and there are many options available if you decide to use them. I know a lot of people like to use them—and particularly those not yet able to stitch; it is a way of achieving a goal. It is also a good opportunity for me to discuss different ways to attach a buckle to a belt.

Be aware that the type of rivets used can have an effect on the performance of the belt, so choosing the right option is important. Let's have a look at those options:

1. Capped rivets: These consist of two parts, the post and cap. The post is slightly crimped toward the top and designed to expand at this point when placed into the cap and struck. They are often made of thin soft metal because they need to bend to work. The issue with capped rivets is we can never see how well the post has expanded inside the cap and how strong the rivet actually is. It is also important to use the correct size rivet to suit the leather you are fixing. Too short and it will not catch properly; too long and the post will buckle, making it ineffective.

2. Saddler rivets: These are most often copper but can be found in brass. They come in two parts, the post and burr (or washer). The burr is placed over the post and tapped down to where it needs to sit. The post is then cut to length and peened over, locking the burr into place. Being able to cut the post to length makes this option very versatile. You can clearly see the workings of the rivet, so you know immediately if it is effective and strong enough. It may not look as pretty, but you can trust them and they will not fail.

3. Chicago screw: If you were wanting to make a belt that allows you to change the buckle quickly, this is an ideal option, and so it is very popular for people with a collection of buckles. It also gives customers the choice of belt and buckle, making it ideal if you attend craft shows or fairs because you can put them together quickly and quietly. It is basically a large-headed screw in two parts, one male, one female, which screw together, securing your strap. They are a popular choice on rifle slings and for gun leather, and have been around for quite some time. They are usually the most expensive option of the four, but they are very strong and, if a thread glue is used, unlikely to fail.

4. Snaps: These are made from four parts and are often found on pouches and small bags. They consist of a post and stud that makes the male part, usually attached to the body, and a cap and socket making the female part, usually attached to the flap. They can be added to a belt to make the buckle removable with just a pull of the leather. Snaps add a little more bulk, but if you are looking to swap-over buckles frequently, it's a good choice as no tools are needed, and they just snap together once the new buckle has been put in place.

If you take a look at the template for the Riveted Belt (p. 43), you'll find, because they all work in a similar fashion, the same template can be used for all the above options.

Be aware that if you intend to make a belt in this style—with the view of changing buckles—one issue you are going to encounter is that the buckles may well vary in size. This throws off using our center hole a little. A way of dealing with this would be to add a few more holes, perhaps nine in total, to give you a little more scope.

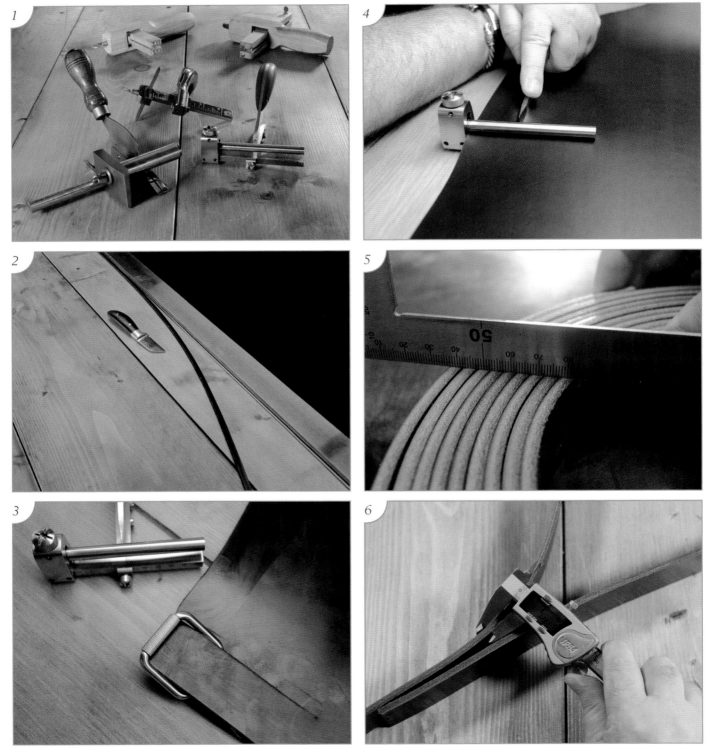

CORE SKILLS
CUTTING

STRAPS

In belt making, unless you are cutting your straps with a knife, there is very little freehand cutting to be done. Everything can be cut with a strap cutter, be it a draw gauge or a plough gauge; even a knife will do the job.

I imagine if you are tackling belts, you are armed with at least some of these.

A plough gauge is certainly an advantage, but if you are on a budget, a wooden strap cutter will serve just as well. It is worth noting that if you do use a proper strap cutter, you run absolutely no risk of undercutting your leather and spoiling the edge of your belt. (1)

A long ruler is also an advantage for getting the first straight edge on your hide. This wants to be done with care, since this edge will set the standard for all straps that come after. (2)

Once you have started your cut, before you go too far it is worth testing it in your buckle. It is very hard to deal with a strap that is even only slightly oversized, so this is a good opportunity to check. (3)

After you have cut the straight edge, use your preferred tool to cut the straps. (4)

Once your strap is cut, a good way to check to see if it is even and consistent is to roll it. Hold a ruler over the top to see if there are any dips or low spots—this is an indication of a narrow area. (5)

When the strap is cut, you need to know if one end is thicker than the other. Ideally, the thick end is the end used for the billet. (6)

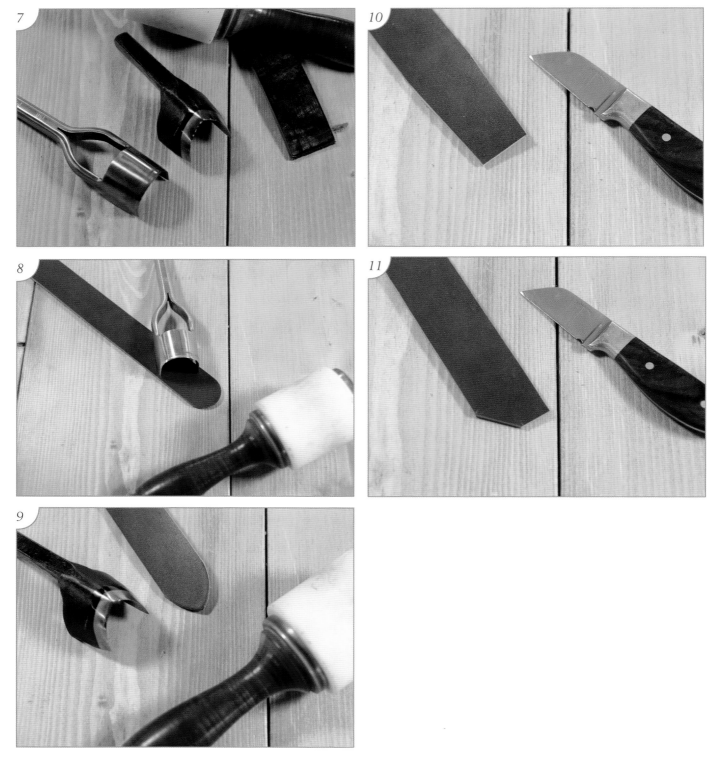

CUTTING BELT TIPS

The next major cut on a belt is the tip. This is normally done once the belt has been measured. The quickest and most effective way of doing so is to use a strap-end punch. It takes a second to do and gives the most consistent cut. (7)

Most punches are limited to the English point or American round, both of which can be achieved with a disk if you don't yet have a punch. The American round requires a disk the same diameter as the width of the belt. (8)

With an English point, a disk twice the size of the width of the belt works very well. (9)

Tapering the tip is also a nice touch. About 60 mm from the tip is a good distance to taper to, but this can be your choice. Measure between 3 to 5 mm in from the edge of the belt and a line drawn to the 60 mm mark. This achieves the taper nicely and makes the belt look rather smart. (10)

Finally, a very simple clipped corner can be quite an effective tip and works well on larger belts. This is as simple as halving the belt width for the measurement; let's say a 50 mm belt for example. So, we would mark 25 mm in from the edge and 25 mm in from the tip, and cut across the corner. The sharp corners can be rounded slightly to soften them, and the result can be quite pleasing. (11)

There are many more ways of doing this, but these are the examples I use in this book.

DRESSING THE LEATHER

Edge dressing is an ideal way to professionally finish the edges of leather, taking the quality up to the next level. This will include creasing, beveling, applying Edge Kote and beeswax, and slicking.

CREASING

All the leather I am using is bridle butt: this resists a crease and so needs heat to achieve a nice line. I shall need to use a screw crease to do this.

This is a skill that needs a lot of practice, especially on curves and corners. It will give me a clean, sharp line into the leather and will be more permanent. The other benefit of hot creasing is that less pressure is needed to apply a line, so more accuracy can be attained. (*1*)

BEVELING

Removing the sharp corners from the leather prevents unnecessary damage and gives the leather a nice, tactile feel. A beveler, named for the result it produces, is used to cut a small strip of leather from the back and front edges, leaving a fine bevel. This makes the edge softer to the touch and less prone to damage. It also makes the edge much easier to dress with edge dye, paint, or ink. (*2*)

SLICKING

After beveling the leather, the fibers at the edge will be rough to the touch and will need bedding in. Applying a solution to the edge of leather will soften the fibers, making them more malleable, thus allowing them to be slicked down. For this you can use water-soluble gum tragacanth or a commercial product such as Tokonole. Once a light solution has been added, the edge can be slicked by applying even pressure and rubbing in line with the edge of the leather. (*3*)

This needs to be done for only as long as it takes for the edge to feel smooth. Too much pressure and the leather will distort; too much rubbing and the edge can dry out and begin to rough up again. (*4*)

SANDING

Once a clean and smooth edge has been achieved, sand it lightly to create a key to which the Edge Kote can adhere. It may seem counterproductive to smooth an edge off just to rough it up again, but having a consistent edge is important, and making it porous is important so the product can adhere to it. (*5*)

EDGE KOTE

Adding a stain or paint to the leather edge not only adds a fine level of detail, it also protects the leather's edge against the elements working with the crease. Once you have chosen your desired product, it is vital that you test it on a small piece of leather. Be careful, because some dyes are not designed for edge work and can bleed into the leather. I like to use Edge Kote because its viscosity is greater than the dye, so it will not penetrate as deep and stain. (*6*)

7

SLICKING

When you have a consistent edge, leave it to dry for a while: it doesn't take long. Once dry, rub the edge with beeswax—you don't need much, just a covering. Having done this, rub with a slicker again. As the beeswax begins to heat up, it bonds with the fibers and Edge Kote and seals them together to give a nice clean edge. A good rub with a cloth to take off any excess wax and you are done. (7)

SPLITTING AND SKIVING

SKIVING MACHINE

Evidently the right tool for the job! But so expensive, and they take an age to master as well as needing a lot of space. If you have one, skiving belts will take you seconds. But be warned: you don't need to take off much to make a big difference. Often just taking 1 mm off a 4 mm strap will change dramatically how the leather bends. Taking off too much can weaken the belt by the buckle. Never take off more than half the depth. I'm not going into any more detail than that. If you have a skiving machine, you should know how it works.

FRENCH SKIVE

If you don't yet have a splitter, a great alternative is a French skive. This tool allows you to take off narrow and thin strips, reducing the bulk of the return in increments. I tend to do this on a belt by starting at the outer edges on the inner end of the slot. (1)

Once the outer strips have been trimmed, I move the tool into the strap and take off the high points. (2)

The secret of this tool lies in the two small bars at the front. They don't let the edge of the tool sink into the leather, to stop you from cutting too deeply. Once the second pass has been completed, there is likely only a center pass needed to even the leather up. (3)

Once done, check the bend of the leather and see how flexible it is now. (4)

If it's bending well, it's done. If not, repeat. A taper can be added by repeating, but this time start halfway down the return. This reduces only half of the return, giving a tapered appearance.(5)

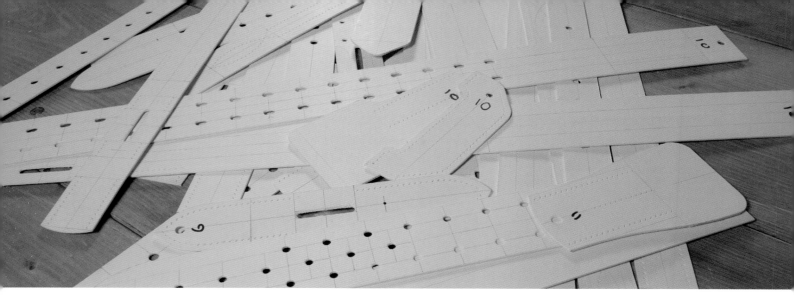

TEMPLATES

I cannot overstate the need for a template.

Belts are seen by too many people as just simple strips of leather, and as such, the idea of making a template for one is just plain silly and a waste of time. We are all entitled to our opinions and have our own views on the subject. Here you are getting mine—you need a template!

A template removes all the guesswork. It makes it easy to measure the belt. It ensures all your stitching—functional or fancy—is in the correct place: that your holes are centered, the keep is square, the tip is in the middle, and you do not have to do any working out on the leather. When you take a knife to your leather, there should be no doubt about what you are doing with it.

It does not matter if you are making one or twenty; templates are an excellent way of building consistency into your work. This consistency is not just about the belts themselves, but also the processes involved. If you can standardize the processes to suit your style, designing becomes a lot easier.

For example, if we were to look at the order of process for the templates for a stitched-in keep belt, we could follow a process similar to this:

Buckle end
1. Cut template to width and add centerline.
2. Curve the return.
3. Add first set of holes.
4. Add first slot line.
5. Add 16 mm slot frame.
6. Add slot.
7. Add second slot line.
8. Add second set of holes.

Billet end
1. Cut template to width and add centerline.
2. Cut tip.
3. Mark 100 mm from tip.
4. Add holes 25 mm apart.

If we follow these steps every time, our consistency increases, and in turn so does our quality.

We can do other things
1. Use the same number of stitches per inch—spi.
2. Set the stitching in from the edge the same distance each time.
3. Set the keep the same distance from the buckle.

Doing this not only begins to build consistency but also builds a signature. Something people can recognize and trust.

THE SLOT!

Which one to use and when?

A very basic and loose rule is that the length of the slot is the same as the width of the belt. This is certainly true for most belts and most buckles. However, in the Ranger Belt (p. 147) you will see me using a 38 mm slot on a 32 mm belt. This was because the buckle's tine was quite heavy, and a 32 mm slot would have been too tight.

Equally, in the Bushcraft Belt (p.1 25), I use 38 mm slots on a 50 mm belt. This was due to the tine being very similar in length and size to that of a 38 mm buckle.

If you have a narrow, thin tine, a short slot will work. If it is thick and heavy, a longer one is needed. It is always worth testing the slot on the buckle before you commit it to your belt.

HOLES

One very simple rule here: use a hole punch that is big enough to go over the tine of your buckle. This will mean the tine will fit the hole you made; it is no more complicated than that.

As for the shape, an oval hole will help the belt sit a little flatter if the leather is thick, but can look a little utilitarian; round holes suit a smarter belt a little better, but this is very much a personal choice.

STITCHING

Stitching is a subject that could fill a whole other book! (Hmm . . . note to self!)

What I am going to cover here are the specific stitching techniques used in belt making.

Trying to teach you stitching in the space I have in this book is an impossible task. So I have to make the assumption that you have, at least, a basic understanding of the saddle stitch. If you are just starting out, and feel that the stitching is a daunting task, this is not an issue. I have a whole channel dedicated to skills, techniques, and projects on my website, and a good number of these are about stitching. Whether you are left- or right-handed, want to stitch in the modern or traditional style, or just looking for the best to suit you, there is something for you there. Check it out.

First, a couple of no-nos.

You will not see me stitch across the strap. This was discouraged in strap making as it was seen as creating a point of weakness—a row of serrations if you like.

However, times change: with the modern leathers being better than they ever were, and the fact that a belt is never really put under that much strain, it is unlikely that these stitch holes would really make a massive difference. Nevertheless, it is frowned upon and seen as a short cut—nearly as much as using rivets. (*1*)
I don't cut a groove for a row of stitching on the front, and very rarely on the back. The grain side of the leather is by far the strongest, so cutting a groove into this and stitching directly against the flesh of the leather is counterproductive. It weakens it, exposes the flesh to the elements, and prevents you achieving a good-looking, angled, saddle stitch. (*2*)

TECHNIQUES
The belts in this book can be stitched using either the traditional or modern methods. If you've been trained or are practiced in the traditional style, you don't need me to explain further. However, I have stitched all the belts in the modern style.

In addition to the basic saddle stitch, the additional techniques employed in this book are shown on the following pages.

THE LOCKING STITCH

1 When stitching right-handed—your first needle is the right-hand needle—you would normally add a cast. This is where you pass the thread up and over the needle to encourage the face thread to sit high, assisting with the angle of the face stitch. If you forget this, the stitch will look flat.

2 When stitching a buckle into place, the leather, which is bent back on itself, keeps trying to pull apart and straighten out. The place this usually occurs is the second-to-last hole since you both approach the buckle and stitch away from it.

3 If you add a single cast, the stitch slips and the leather opens. If you add not one but four casts, this causes the thread to twist around itself inside the bend and lock.

4 When a little tension is applied, the twists pull in toward the middle of the bend.

5 As you apply more tension, the leather is pulled together, and because of the twists, it doesn't pull apart. The thread, which needs to be waxed, locks against itself and keeps everything in place. This is usually done on both sides; first as you approach the buckle, and then as you begin stitching away from the buckle. If you have a particularly thick keep, the same can be done when stitching that in too.

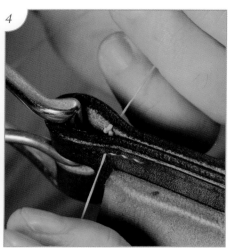

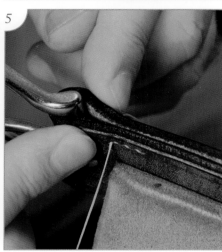

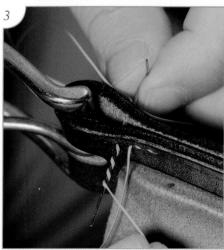

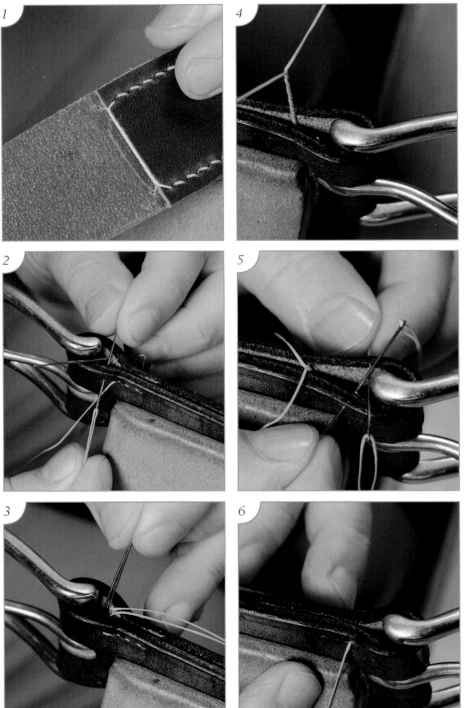

TWISTS

1 When stitching a strap, belt, collar, or such, twisting can be done with one thread.

It is a case of passing the thread from one side of the strap to the other. In the past, this was done by way of a twist, which was exposed at the end of the return.

2 To prevent unnecessary wear on this thread, it can now be passed down inside of the bend behind the buckle. It does the same job but is far more protected.

To achieve this, stop your row of stitching at the second-to-last hole—the hole where you add the locking stitch. Then pass the two needles from the outside to the inside through the last hole.

3 Once the needles are on the inside, pass them through the bend to the other side. Make sure you do not inadvertently pass them through the loop of the tine.

4 Once the needles have been passed to the other side, turn the belt over in the clam.

The threads should now be poking up out of the bend. Begin to twist them together—how much depends on your thread, but ten twists per every half inch is a good measure. Twist your threads until they begin to sit up above the leather.

5 Once you have sufficient twists, pass the needles from the inside to the outside.

Which needle is which is not important; you will only add one more twist or drop one, which will have little impact. The idea of the twist is to transfer the tension from one side of the belt to the other and keep the threads taut.

6 With the needles now on the outside, you can continue stitching toward yourself. The first stitch will take you to the second hole, where you will apply the locking stitch with the four casts. This ensures that the leather has been caught at the same place, in the same way, on both sides.

FANCY STITCH

Adding a fancy stitch is a lot simpler than it looks and makes a strong visual impact. It is a case of stitching between two fixed points, lots of times. (1)

This image was drawn using a 100 mm curve intersecting the centerline at the same point. This is the design used on the Ranger Belt (p.147), so it is calculated for a belt 32 mm wide, which has a row of stitching set in at 5 mm. Alter the curve from 100 to 75 mm and the look changes quite a bit. (2)

This is a different design but made the same way; it is made just by using a smaller disc and not overlapping the curve. Adding a bit of straight stitching in between changes it again. (3)

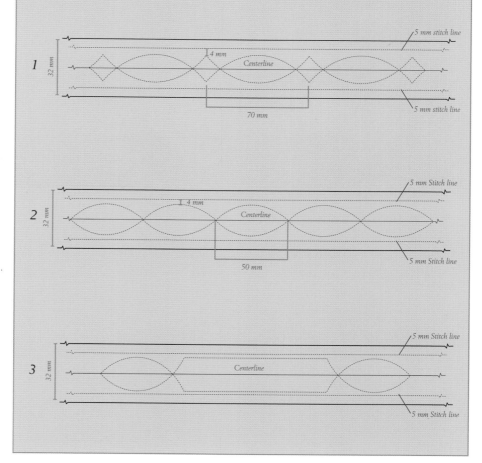

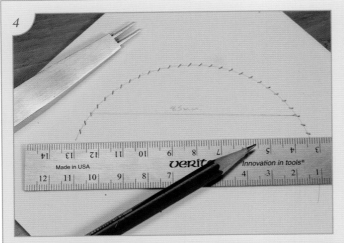

You can be as elaborate as you wish, and there are a great many designs that can be added quite simply. The one thing to remember is to not have a long or short stitch. This is very simple to achieve.

- Draw a curve on a piece of card, using the desired disk.

- Add a row of stitching to this line, slightly longer than needed.

- Now measure the distance between the holes that will be used, and this will give you the perfect stitch line on each curve. (4)

This will ensure a nice cross at each of the intersections. In the past, I've made the holes with standard irons on one side and reverse on the other; this gives a nice clean cross, making the design very sharp. (5)

This is what the fancy stitching can look like on a belt (6).

CALCULATING THREAD LENGTH

Running out of thread, or playing thread chicken as it will now be called, is everyone's fear when stitching a large item. No one wants an unnecessary tangle of back stitches spoiling a nice stitch line, but how do we avoid this?

There are many who offer advice that ranges from using four times the length of stitching all the way up to ten. Luckily, working out how much thread you need is not difficult.

On my website, I have a free downloadable sheet that assists with this.

Work out how long your stitching is. To keep the math simple, we will call this 1 meter or 1,000 mm. This is how much thread you can actually see once the item is stitched. There are two sides, so we are up to 2,000 mm already.

We need to know how many holes we have; let's say we are stitching at 3.85 mm (7 spi): this will be 1,000 ÷ 3.85 = 260. So 260 holes.

Our leather is 5 mm, so we would use this sum: 5 × 260 = 1,300. This is how much thread we can't see; it's in the holes. Of course, this is times two since there are two threads, so double.

Finally, we need to ensure that there is enough thread left over for the back stitches, plus something to hang onto to finish off, and for this we add 250 mm to each needle.

Putting all this together, our calculation should look like this:

Hole count	260
Leather thickness	5 mm
Face thread	1,000 mm
Back thread	1,000 mm
Internal thread 1	1,300 mm
Internal thread 2	1,300 mm
Tail 1	250 mm
Tail 2	250 mm
Total	**5,100 mm**

On this occasion, five times our stitching length is required to stitch in one go. Vary the thickness of the leather or the spi, and this will change. This calculation works for any stitch length on any item and is a really good chart to have to hand.

The leather you are stitching will have an impact: softer leather will tension more so need less; firm or hard leather will tension less, but the above calculator will still work since it is set for very firm leather.

One final thing to remember . . . it is always better to have more thread than not enough. So round up, rather than shorten, a long thread.

YEOMAN'S BELT

Vintage is definitely in, with more people asking for older-style belts, so I thought this was a good example to include. The design of this belt likely dates back to 1903. It was manufactured for the British military and widely issued during World War I. Its charm is in its simplicity: there's no stitching! So no thread to rot and very little else to fail. It was cheap to make and could be done by unskilled labor in large volumes.

Belts had been stitched for thousands of years prior to this; the design and lack of stitching were very intentional and based on the simplicity of production and its durability.

When worn, it is as useful and as strong as any stitched belt of similar design.

I have included it because it's an excellent place to begin if you are just starting out, because it's a very achievable item to make with minimal tools. Furthermore, the design of buckle can be changed, and you can build up your stitching skills, so the belt can grow with you, as it were.

The construction could not be simpler. It's a strip of leather, with two holes at one end and nine at the other. The buckle is a center bar held in place in one of the two holes, with a riveted keep holding everything tidy. The reason for the two holes and them being so far apart was that the second hole was used as a matter of course. The first hole made the belt bigger so that in cold weather it could be worked around a jerkin or greatcoat.

Commonly, the leather was not creased, beveled, or dressed, but there are examples of this belt where this has been done. How far you go with yours is entirely up to you. I am keeping the design as close as possible to the original but will be adding a bevel and creasing it. I'll leave the edge natural but slicked down slightly.

TOOLS & MATERIALS

6 mm hole punch	Pencil	**Leather:** Printed dry butt
Beveler	Ruler	**Buckle:** 2 in. center bar
Card	Ruler stop	**Rivets:** Saddlers' rivets
Cloth	Saddlers rivets + setter	
Coin (a penny)	Slicker	
Crease	Snips	
Cutting edge	Template knife	
Hammer or maul		

1 This belt was first made when imperial measurements were being used in the industry. So, for fun, we are going to make it using inches and feet. It could be said that this belt is simple enough to make without the need of a template—we're not the sort to say that sort of thing though, are we?

Let's start with our card. The belt will be 2 in. wide, so I have two strips of card, 2 in. wide and 16 in. long. I have drawn a centerline down each.

2 Starting with the buckle template, I have rounded off the two corners with a penny and marked 4 in. and 6 in. in from the end; these will be the two holes for the buckle to sit in. That's the buckle template done!

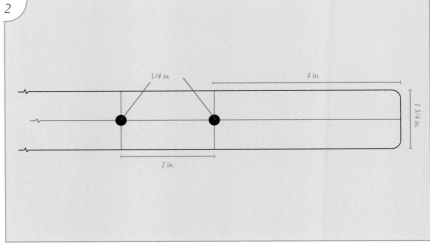

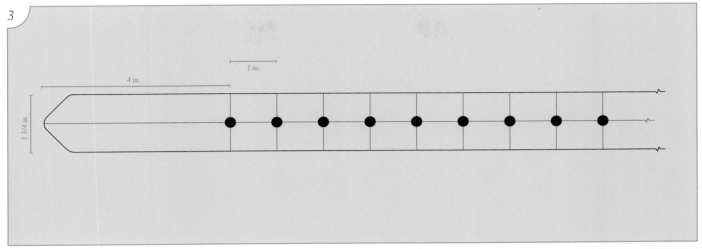

3

1 in.

4 in.

1 3/4 in.

3 So far, all we have needed for tools is a ruler, a scratch awl, a penny, a knife, a hole punch, and a hammer.

The billet end is not that much more complex. I have cut the tip, using two straight lines at 45 degrees each: this is a 90-degree cut. The sharp edges will be rounded with the coin and knife. I have then marked in 4 in. from the tip for the first hole and eight more holes at 1 in. increments.

4 With the templates made, we can now go to our leather. Cut a strip of your chosen leather 2 in. wide—I used bridle butt.

5 You may notice that the leather has a thin and thick end; the thin end wants to be under the buckle. Place the buckle template over the thin end and mark where the two holes will sit.

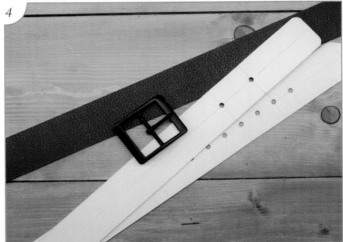

4

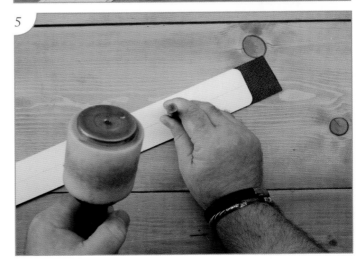

5

6 While this is not known as a fitted belt, there's no reason we can't make it so. Lay the strap out straight with the buckle template over the buckle end, and line the 0 (zero) up with the second hole. Put a rule or tape next to the strap and place the billet template over the top of the leather, line up the center hole (hole 5) next to the measurement you want the belt to be. In my case it is 40 in.

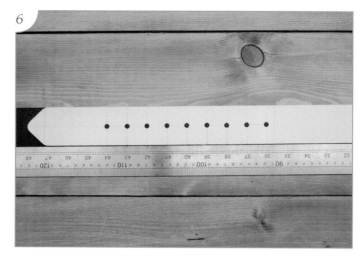

7 Mark the tip and all of the holes at your billet end ready for cutting and punching.

Once all the holes and ends have been marked, we can begin to cut the strap to size, starting with the buckle end.

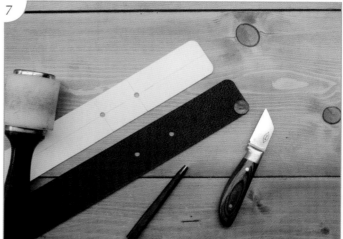

8 Once this is done, we will move to the billet end; I have cut the tip with a ruler and rounded the corners and tip with a penny and knife. Once this is done, punch all the holes through.

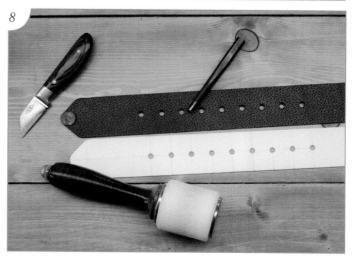

9 Next is the keep. This wants to be a strip of leather about ¾ in. wide; it needs to be long enough so it wraps around two layers of the belt and fully overlaps itself on the back, and this is about 4 in. We haven't made a template for this; it is simple enough that we can go straight to the leather.

10 All our pieces have been cut and are almost ready to use. I am adding a crease; this will just present it a little better but was not always done to this type of belt. I have creased the face of the belt and both sides of the keep.

11 Following on from the crease, I am beveling the entire edge of the belt, both back and front, as well as the keep.

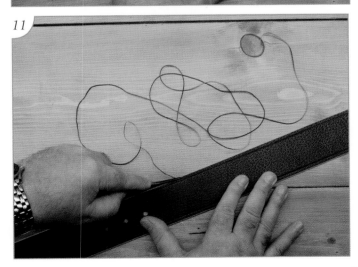

12 Finally, I'm dressing the edge with some Tokonole and burnishing it with a piece of canvas. Historically, if this was done to this type of belt, something akin to "gum arabic" may well have been used.

13 To finish, a couple of rivets need to be added to the keep. I am using saddlers copper rivets for this in 14 g. One is more than enough; however, two looks better.

I marked one end of the keep at ½ in. and 1¼ in., where the rivets will sit. Then I punched two small holes in the keep, big enough for the rivets.

14 Now bend the keep around two layers of the belt, with the holes you have just made on top; mark through to the other layer where the holes need to be made. Punch through once marked.

15 With the holes made, put the posts through both ends of the keep, with the burrs over the top, and tap down. Snip off any excess.

Peen over the end of the post so it is rounded and has no sharp edges (*inset*). I have a specific tool for this, but a ball head or peening hammer can be used.

Your belt is complete! All that is left to do now is to add the buckle to your preferred hole at the buckle end of the strap—I used the second hole. Add the keep and it's ready for use.

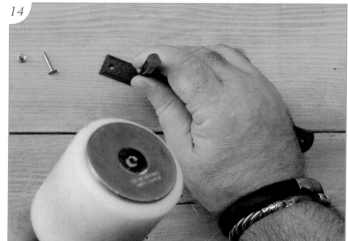

RIVETED BELT

I'm not a fan of rivets here in the workshop; all the items I make are stitched. That's because I trust my stitching and guarantee it, but I cannot say the same for rivets. I know there are many who prefer the use of rivets, so for those and the ones not yet able to stitch well enough, it is a way of achieving a goal.

TOOLS & MATERIALS

100 mm disk	Pencil	**Leather:** Black bridle butt
3 mm and 6 mm hole punches	Rivets and setter	**Buckle:** 1½ in. Westend steel
Beveler	Ruler	**Keep:** Flat cast steel
Card	Ruler stop	**Rivets:** Tubular rivet, closed stem
Creaser	Scratch awl	
Crew punch (oblong or bag punch)	Skiving knife	
Cutting edge	Slicker	
Dividers	Strap end punch / 2.9 in. (75 mm)	
Hammer or maul	disk	
Knife		

1 Working to a belt width of 38 mm, we will need two templates: one for the buckle end and one for the billet.

Cut two strips of card 38 mm wide 400 mm long and add a centerline down the length. Cut a curve to one end with a 100 mm) disk to give a nice finish to the inside of the belt. Your template should look something like this.

2 The template consists of little more than a series of holes; nonetheless, placement of those holes needs to be consistent. As with all belts, there is a point at which it folds—the bar line. The bar line works the same for both heel bar and center bar buckles and is usually located at the center of the slot made to accept the tine or prong.

Working from the rounded end, place the holes 8 mm in from the edge of the card on both sides; this is to the center of the hole. Add holes at 8, 38, 96, and 126 mm—eight holes in total.

The slot is set 10 mm in from the inner holes, with one end of the slot starting at 48 mm and ending at 86 mm. The inner holes will keep the buckle in place, and the outer will secure the keep.

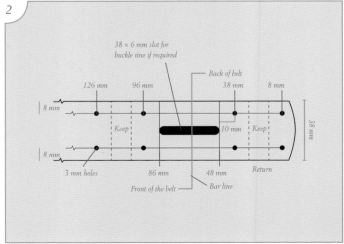

3 This template is designed for all buckles, but if you are making a belt exclusively for trophy buckles, you don't need the slot and can shorten the distance between the inner holes a little. Here is an example to assist.

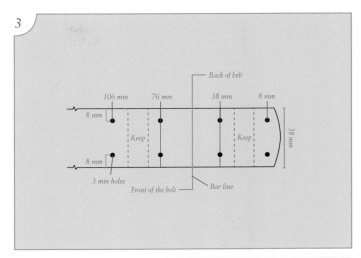

4 Now to the template for the billet end. This time I'm using an English point, although, of course, you can choose whichever end you wish.

In most cases, the distance from the first hole and the end of the belt is about 100 mm, with the distance between the holes being 25 mm. The holes need to be an uneven number so that the buckle can be centered when worn.

Cut your card 38 mm wide and 400 mm long, add the tip, and draw a centerline.

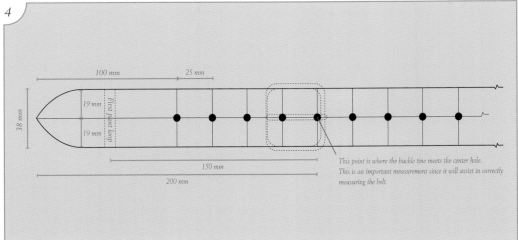

5 Mark 100 mm from the tip and draw a line across the template; this gives you the position for the first hole. Now draw eight more lines 25 mm apart to give a total of nine lines. The center of the hole we need to make lies at the points where these lines cross the centerline.

Take a hole punch big enough to fit over the tine of the buckle you intend to use. I used a 6 mm punch and punched out all nine holes.

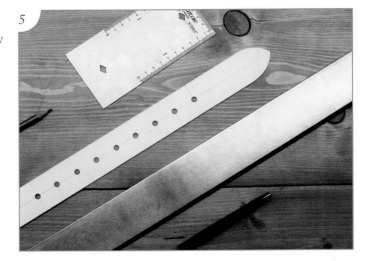

6 Referring back to the issue you may encounter with different buckle sizes for a moment; as you progress through the projects, you will see that a measuring point is added to the templates when we know the buckle sizes we are working with.

This makes it much easier to make a belt precise when making a belt to measure.

In this instance, I am using a buckle that measures 38 mm from the heel bar to the point where the tine meets the roller. In view of this, I'll go back to my buckle template and add a mark 38 mm from the centerline on the return.

7 With the templates made, cut a strap 38 mm wide from your chosen leather. Here I used black bridle butt in 4.5 mm. As always, the easiest end on the belt to mess up is the buckle end, so this is the place to start. Place the buckle end template over one end of your strap, and mark the curved cut with a scratch awl. Then press through the template with the crew and hole punches to mark the leather.

8 Punch out all the holes and cut the curve at the end of the strap. If everything is centered and looks good, move forward. If something is misaligned, move the template down a little and start again; this is why the strap isn't cut to length before the difficult bit has been mastered.

9
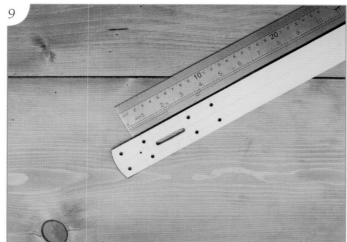

10
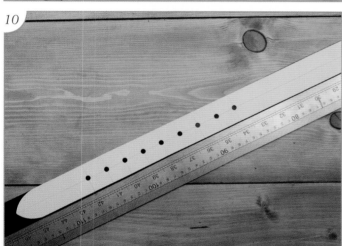

11
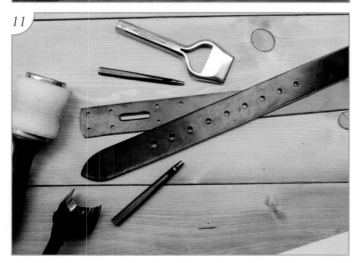

12
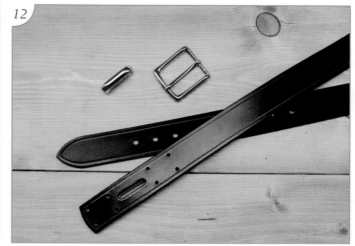

9 Now measure the belt. Place the buckle template back onto the leather over where it's just been worked, and line a ruler up so 0 (zero) is on the measuring point.

10 Place the billet end of the template over the strap at the other end, and line up the measuring mark with the center hole to suit the measurement you want. I marked this one at 965 mm.

11 With the billet end template placed in the correct position to suit the measurement, mark the end of the belt—here, I'm using an English point and nine holes. The strap can now be cut to length and the holes made.

12 The belt is now cut to length, and all the holes have been made, so it's now time to dress the leather. Even if we are taking a shortcut on attaching the buckle, we can still take the time to make the leather look good. I added a crease to it, beveled the edge to give it a rounded feel, and applied Edge Kote and beeswax to dress the edges. The strap is now done.

13 It's almost time to add the hardware, but before we do so we need to remove some of the bulk from the back of the leather, so it doesn't feel too thick or heavy. You do not need to take off much to make a difference. Usually, the skive begins prior to the slot, and if you have one, a splitter is an ideal way to get a consistent edge. If you don't yet have a splitter, a great alternative is a French skive. I used the French skive for this belt. Starting at the outside edges, I took off a light strip of leather no more than 1 mm thick.

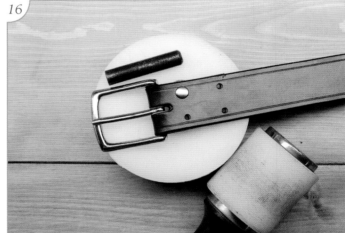

14 Having skived the two outer strips, move toward the middle of the leather, taking the high point off in strips. This will give an even finish on the back, reducing the bulk and tapering the strap nicely.

15 By making these cuts, the unfinished leather is left exposed. Treat this area with some conditioner or balm of your choice, to preserve the leather.

16 The belt is almost finished. It is now a case of adding the hardware to finish it off.

Start with the buckle. Slide the buckle over the strap, ensuring it is the right way around, and place the tine in the slot and fold the leather over.

17 Using your rivet of choice—here I used capped rivets—place them in the two holes closest to the buckle.

Set the rivets in place that will hold the buckle. Slide the keep over the strap into place behind the next set of holes, ensuring that it is trapped between the main body of the belt and the return. With this in place, the second set of rivets can be added in the same way as the first (*inset*).

Your belt is now complete. Try it on and see how it fits. This is a much quicker way of making a belt, and many belt sellers use this method to save time and effort. By all means give it a go, but consider working through the stitched projects in this book to raise the level of the belts you make.

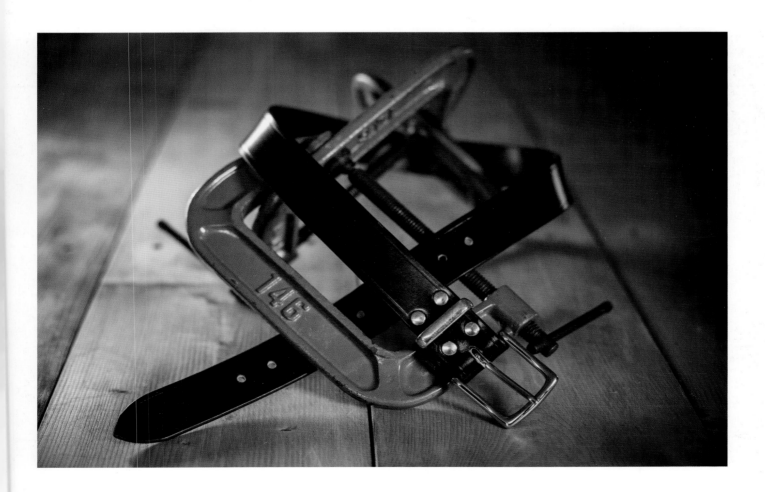

MEASURING BELT

A well-made measuring belt is an almost foolproof way of measuring a customer for a bespoke belt: this is the Armitage leather-belt-measuring thing!

Sizing a belt often brings difficulties. I am frequently given a waist size that may or may not be current, or a waist size the customer believes—or wishes—they had. This is of little help, and it's frustrating to be told once the belt is made that it doesn't fit. Waist size and belt size are not the same, and this is where the issue lies. So, we are going to look at a foolproof resolution to make correct size belts every time.

For ease of use, this belt will end up providing measurements in inches, although the workings are in metric.

TOOLS & MATERIALS

6 mm hole punch	Number stamping set	**Leather:** Natural tooling butt
Beveler	Pencil	**Buckle:** 1½ in. Westend roller steel
Card	Ruler	**Thread:** Tiger, white 0.6 mm
Crease	Ruler stop	
Crew punch (oblong or bag punch)	Scratch awl	
Cutting edge	Skiving knife	
Disk	Slicker	
Dividers	Strap end punch	
Hammer or maul	Stitching irons	
Knife	Slicker	

1 This belt is designed to be tried on by a customer of an as yet-unknown size. As such, I have kept the strap full length and will keep cutting to a minimum, if possible. My strap is currently 1.75 m long.

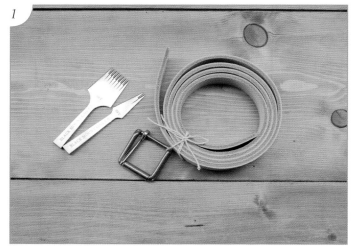

2 Two templates are needed to make this belt, one for the buckle end and one for the billet end. This is not a fitted belt; we are making it as long as possible and will be adding as many holes as we can. In view of this, cut two strips of card, both 38 mm wide: one long at 840 mm, and one short at 200 mm.

Add a centerline to both pieces of card, cut a curve to one end of the short template, and cut an English point at one end of the long.

3 Start with the buckle template. I intend to add only a short row of stitching. No keep is required, since the belt is not going to be worn as a belt, but only tried on to find the correct size.

In view of this, the stitching does not need to be long, and no gap is needed for a keep, so I add twelve holes for the stitching at 7 spi (3.85 mm).

The illustration shows what the template should look like. I have used a 100 mm disk to round off one end and added two 5 mm stitch lines to either side.

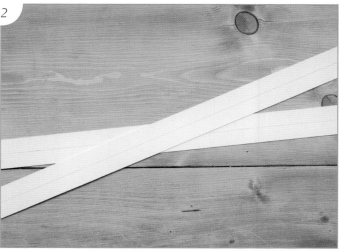

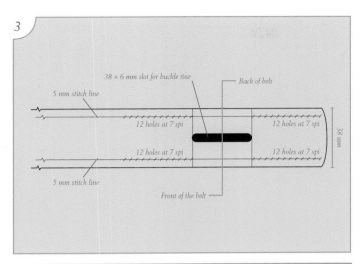

3

38 × 6 mm slot for buckle tine ——— Back of belt

5 mm stitch line

12 holes at 7 spi — *12 holes at 7 spi* — 38 mm

12 holes at 7 spi — *12 holes at 7 spi*

5 mm stitch line

Front of the belt ———

4 The position of the slot for the tine is dictated by the length of stitching. I start by placing one tooth of the iron over the edge of the leather. This sets the first hole one full stitch from the edge of the leather. I then lightly tap the iron to mark where the holes will sit.

5 This is then repeated on the opposite side of the card. Once you have two sets of holes, draw a line at a right angle at the end of the two rows. This will be one end of the slot for the tine.

6 Draw the frame to help place the punch to the template. Most punches are 6 mm wide; this belt is 38 mm wide, so if we remove the 6 mm, we are left with 32 mm. Half this, and we have 16 mm. Draw a 16 mm line from the edge of the card where the slot is going to sit, and we have the frame in which we can place the punch centered to the template.

4

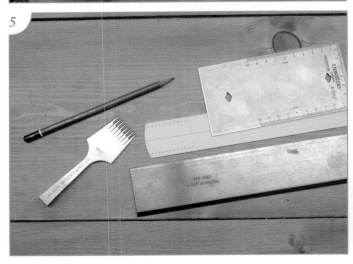

5

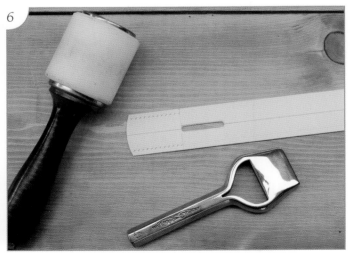

6

7 At the other end of the slot, add a further line at a right angle to the card. This is now where the rest of the holes will be added. Line up your iron, with the first tooth touching this line and sitting on the 4 mm stitch line. Strike and make your holes—do this on both sides. You should now have four sets of holes and a slot for the buckle tine.

8 Measure the distance between the two lines at either end of the slot; this should be about 38 mm. Draw a line vertically halfway between them. This is the bar line and the point at which the leather will bend from the front to the back.

As a very loose rule, the width of most buckles is the same as the distance from the heel bar to where the tine meets the roller. If this is the case for your buckle, measure 38 mm from the centerline you have just drawn toward the back of the template on the return, and make a small hole or mark. This mark represents where the hole of the belt meets the tine of the buckle and our first measuring point.

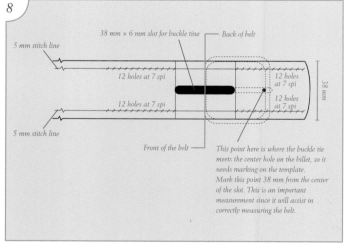

5 mm stitch line

38 mm × 6 mm slot for buckle tine — Back of belt

12 holes at 7 spi

12 holes at 7 spi

12 holes at 7 spi

12 holes at 7 spi

38 mm

5 mm stitch line

Front of the belt —

This point here is where the buckle tie meets the center hole on the billet, so it needs marking on the template. Mark this point 38 mm from the center of the slot. This is an important measurement since it will assist in correctly measuring the belt.

9 Using this point, we can measure from it to set our holes with some accuracy. Your template should now look something like this.

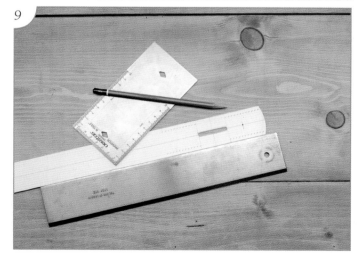

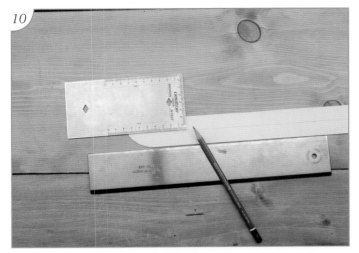

10 Now for the billet template. As before with the buckle one, I have added the centerline and prepared the end, this time with an English point. The billet end does not have to be held by a keep or pant loop, so the distance from the tip to the first hole is not so much of an issue; I am setting my first hole 75 mm from the tip.

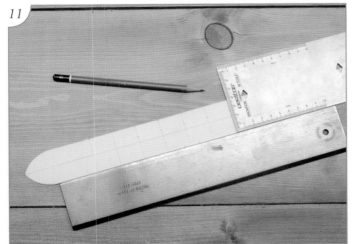

11 Starting at the 75 mm—3 in.—mark from the tip, I set my holes 25 mm—1 in.—apart, and adding as many as the card allows, I will end up with twenty-nine holes using the length of card I have. I mark every 25 mm and add a line covering the width of the card. This forms a cross, making it easier to place the hole punch more accurately.

12 Once the marks have been made, it is time to make the holes. The hole punch needs to be of sufficient size to allow the tine of the buckle to run freely. It is therefore a good idea to choose a hole punch that sits over the buckle tine. I used a 5 mm punch.

13 The holes are not numbered yet, since this will be dictated by the overall length of the strap; however, they will be added later.

14 Place the buckle template on one end of the strap, with a ruler next to it and 0 lined up with the measuring point.

15 Next, line the holes on the billet template as close to the end of the strap as you can get it.

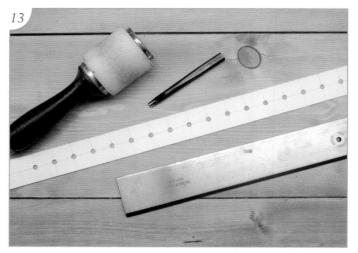

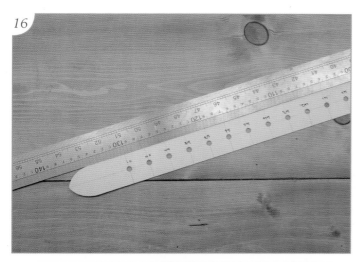

16 You can now begin to see how the numbering of the holes is going to work. The farthest hole near to the tip of the belt is 1.3 m—51 inches—with the closest being 610 mm—24 inches.

The holes can now be marked backward from 51 down to 24. This is an excellent way to get the correct measurement for a customer. Once happy with the count, I add the numbers to my template.

17 With the details worked out, we can now begin to work on the leather. Without doubt, the easiest part to mess up is the slot—in view of this, that's where I begin.

Place the buckle template over one end of the strap, as close to the end as possible, so we get the most from it. With the template centered, place the crew punch into the slot and give it a firm strike. Do not try to punch the slot out through the template; this will destroy it—just strike hard enough to mark the leather, then remove the template and punch all the way through.

18 Now in place, the slot becomes a great locator for the template. Position the template back over the leather, and mark where the stitch holes need to sit, and the curve at the end of the strap. Then cut the end of the strap and make all the stitch holes.

19 Time to mark the holes; place the buckle template back onto the leather and add the billet template to the other end. I have established that the farthest hole I can make is 51 in. (1.3 m) from the measuring point, so this is the hole I'm going to start with.

Normally, we would start at the center hole; however, in this case we are trying to get a strap as long as possible, so we're going to start at the end of the strap itself for the first measurement. Mark all the holes through the template onto the leather strap, along with the tip you have chosen.

20 Once all the holes have been marked and the end of the strap has been cut, we are ready to mark all the numbers. I'm using a Hex n Hit set to mark my numbers, although any number stamp set will do the job.

The leather being used is unfinished russet, so I am lightly dampening it with water to help the stamp mark the leather better. I do this until the leather has an even color, then leave it to dry for twenty minuets.

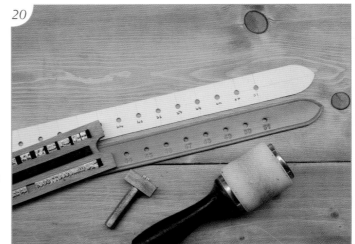

Dress your belt any way you wish. I have added a crease and just given the edges a rub. The stitching is very simple on this belt: two rows and no keeps.

Finally, stitch your chosen buckle into place, and the belt is done.

Numbering the holes like this is a little time-consuming, but it needs doing only once and makes a great tool to have in the workshop.

We have now produced a belt that will fit both the slender and the robust figure equally well, giving you an absolutely accurate measurement to work to.

PLAIN BELT—
LOOSE KEEP

This is the belt that is most likely to be a regular in your repertoire, simpler than the stitched-in keep version but leaps and bounds ahead of what we have done so far.

When finished, if a leather keep has been used, it is difficult to see if the keep has been stitched-in or not; it looks very similar and is evidently a great choice if using a metal keep.

TOOLS & MATERIALS

6 mm hole punches	Knife	**Leather:** Dark Havana bridle butt
Beveler	Pencil	**Buckle:** 1½ in. Bristol brass
Card	Ruler	**Thread:** Tiger, black 0.6 mm
Crease	Ruler stop	**Keep:** Strip-formed belt loop
Crew punch (oblong or bag punch)	Scratch awl	
Cutting edge	Skiving knife	
Disk	Slicker	
Dividers	Strap end punch	
Hammer or maul	Stitching irons	

1 This requires two templates, one for the billet and another for the buckle end. This means it is adjustable when measuring the strap for the belt.

This is the layout for the buckle end. The gaps allow for the addition of a metal keep and make stitching the belt much easier.

I pre-prick all the holes to ensure accuracy with a nine-tooth and a five-tooth iron in 7 spi (3.85 mm), punching all the way though to open the holes up.

Use what irons you have, but keep to the twelve and five hole ratio. This may change for you if you use different irons, but it will still work as long as you achieve the correct symmetry. Using this process requires no initial measurements, since the stitching sets these out as you go. We know that it will need a 20 mm gap for the keep and a 38 mm slot for the buckle, but these are added as we go.

2 Starting at one end, slightly round your template. It can be left straight if you wish, but it is a nice way to finish the back of your belt. Now add two stitch lines 5 mm from the edge of the card on either side.

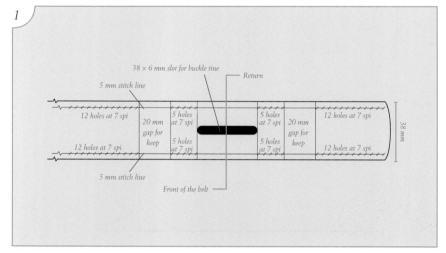

3 The order of what we need to add to our template is as follows: twelve holes, 20 mm gap, five holes, 38 mm gap, five holes, 20 mm gap, twelve holes. Start with the first set of holes. Place one tooth of the long iron over the edge of the card and begin to mark your first set of holes. This will ensure that the last hole is one full stitch from the end of the leather.

4 Mark and make the first row of twelve; mark a line at the end of this row and a line 20 mm farther on—this will be your keep gap. It will be enough for most keeps, since they tend to be about 12.5 mm wide, but check yours before you move forward and adjust if necessary.

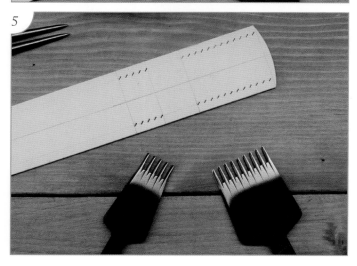

5 After the 20 mm gap, add a further five holes and draw a further line at the end of these. This will be the first line for the slot. Add the holes to the other side of the template, making sure they are all in line.

6 We are now at the point where we need to add the slot for the prong. A loose rule is that the length of the slot is the same as the width of the belt, so in this case 38 mm. Mark a line at the end of the five holes and another 38 mm farther on, and punch your slot out with the crew punch.

7 The front of the belt is a mirror of what we have just done on the back—five holes, 20 mm gap, and twelve holes.

8 The template needs one more mark, a point that we can measure from when laying out the leather. Most 38 mm buckles tend to be almost square, so we need a measurement of 38 mm from the center of the slot toward the back of the belt. This mark will represent where the buckle prong sits on the bar, and also where it meets the center hole of the belt when worn. The diagram shows the outline of a buckle and where this hole should sit.

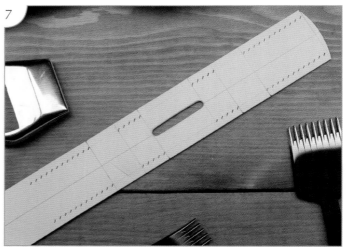

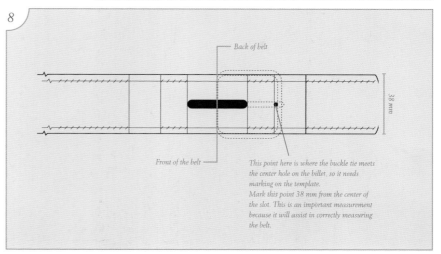

Back of belt

38 mm

Front of the belt —

This point here is where the buckle tie meets the center hole on the billet, so it needs marking on the template.
Mark this point 38 mm from the center of the slot. This is an important measurement because it will assist in correctly measuring the belt.

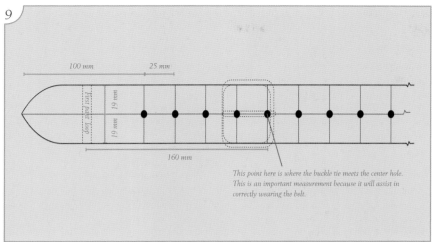

100 mm   25 mm

first part 'loop'

19 mm   19 mm

19 mm

160 mm

This point here is where the buckle tie meets the center hole.
This is an important measurement because it will assist in
correctly wearing the belt.

9 With the template for the buckle end taken care of, we now need to look at the billet end. In most cases, the distance between the first hole and the end of the belt is about 100 mm, with the distance between the holes being 25 mm.

Ideally, the number of holes needs to be an odd number so the buckle can be centered when worn. The reason for this is that when a measured belt is worn on the center hole, the billet is caught under both the keep and the first belt loop of the pants, which is usually about 150 mm off-center.

10 Decide on the design you want the belt tip to be—I've chosen an English point.

Mark 100 mm from the tip and draw a line; now draw eight more lines 25 mm apart. The point where each line crosses the centerline is where the holes need to be. Take a hole punch big enough to fit over the tine of the buckle.

11 Punch all the holes in the template.

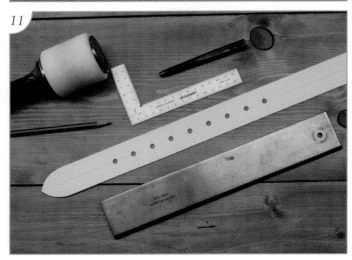

12 Both templates are now complete. This is by far the longest part of making a belt.

However, when a good template has been made, it only needs to be made once. When you take the template to the strap, there's no guesswork, no working out measurements on the leather, and no marking the leather unnecessarily. Everything will come together rather easily, and that is what we will do next.

You will need a strip of leather 38 mm wide. If you are using bridle leather, it is likely to be about 1.5 m long.

13 First, *do not* cut the strap to length! If the strap is too long, leave it so. Most mistakes are made at the buckle end, and if you have already cut the strap to length and made a mistake, you have nowhere to go. Lay the template for the buckle end over the strap. If you are able to hold it down with some weights, even better.

14 The hardest thing to get right is the slot, so mark this first. Place the crew punch over the template and give a single firm strike to mark the leather. Remove the template and ensure the slot is straight. If it is, replace the crew punch without the template and strike through.

12

13

14

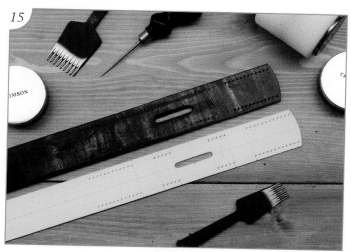

15 If this worked, you can move forward; if it has twisted and is off-line, you have potentially only wasted 125 mm of leather, so you can cut the error off and try again.

Once you have successfully made the slot, replace the template to line up with the edges of the strap and slot; now mark all of your holes. This is also a good opportunity to mark and cut the end of the strap.

16 Now the two templates come into their own. When you measured yourself for a belt, you will have recorded the measurement; let's call it 965 mm to use as an example. Lay the strap out flat on the bench and place the two templates over the top, next to a long ruler.

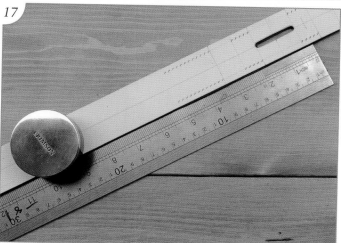

17 Lay the buckle template back on the buckle end of the strap, and line the start of the long ruler, or 0 (zero), up against the measuring point on the buckle template.

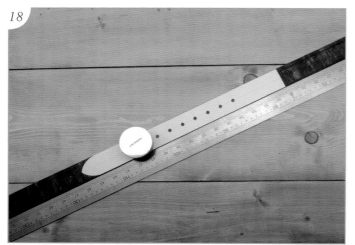

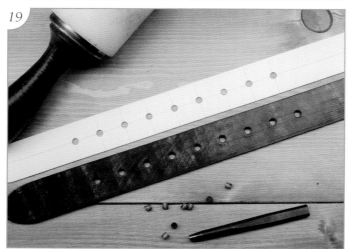

18 Now place the billet template onto the strap so the center hole lines up with 965 mm of the long ruler.

19 Hold down the template with weights so you can mark the holes and the end of the strap for cutting. Using this process will ensure the correct length belt every time if your waist measurements are correct. Cut the strap end and make all your holes—the strap is now almost a belt.

20 If you are able, skiving down the back of the belt is a good idea to remove some of the bulk. This will make it easier to bend the strap to stitch it, and more comfortable to wear. If you are not confident enough of your skill, leave it for now. A skiving knife or splitter is the ideal tool for this job, but I appreciate these may be skills you will want to work up to first.

21 Once the strap is cut to length, all the holes are made, and the strap is thinned down on the back, it's time to dress the belt. A crease is a nice way to finish the edges, but if you are using bridle leather, the creasing iron will need to be hot.

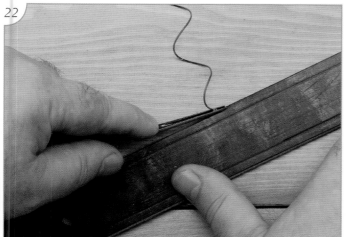

22 Have a good practice with the tool first on some scrap pieces, then apply a crease to the edge of the leather. Once creased, bevel all the edges.

23 Apply whichever solution you prefer to slick the edges down. I used Tokenol. Slick until a nice even sheen has been achieved, lightly sand, apply Edge Kote and beeswax, and slick again.

24 Time to stitch the buckle into the strap. Put the buckle between the leather, ensuring it is the right way around, and fold the leather into place. Line the holes up with a couple of needles and place it in the clam.

25 In this example it's best to stitch toward the buckle. Start with the third hole back in the row of five holes, ready for your two backstitches. There are five holes, so there will be only four stitches. Stitch to the fourth hole only. Once you have stitched to the fourth hole, put the front needle into the fifth hole but make it come out between the two pieces of leather.

26 Do the same for the back needle. Now with both needles sitting between the two pieces of leather, pass the needles through to the other side, ensuring you do not get tangled in the buckle. Turn the piece over in the clam, twist the threads twenty-five times, and push them both out from the inside to the outside in the first hole.

Continue stitching in this position and then finish off with two backstitches.

27 Once the buckle has been stitched in, apply the keep.

28 You can now stitch the rows of twelve holes in the same way; stitch toward the keep, pass the needles through to the middle, then through to the other side, twist, turn, take the needles from inside to out, and continue stitching.

Once you have completed stitching the keep in, the belt is complete. Step back and admire.

PLAIN BELT—
STITCHED KEEP

This is a more advanced belt and one that can be made a number of ways. Traditionally, an awl would have been needed to achieve a belt of this caliber. Today, however, thanks to the development of new irons, we are able to pre-prick the leather, both the belt and the keep.

This has made the process of making a stitched-in keep belt more accessible to more people, and this is the process we are going to be following in this project.

The familiarity of the templates will begin to show here, but we are going to change this design a little. First and foremost because the stitching is in one long run, and second because it features a tapered tip.

TOOLS & MATERIALS

6 mm hole punch	Pencil	**Leather:** *Sedgwick plain butt Windsor oak*
Beveler	Ruler	**Buckle:** *1½ in. swelled Westend roller,*
Card	Ruler stop	*brass*
Crease	Scratch awl	**Thread:** *Tiger, yellow 0.6 mm*
Crew punch (oblong or bag punch)	Skiving knife	
Cutting edge	Slicker	
Disk	Stitching clam	
Dividers	Stitching irons	
Hammer or maul	Strap cutter	
Knife	Strap end punch	

1 Start with the templates. I have two strips of 1.5 mm thick, stiff card, 400 mm long and 38 mm wide, and have run a centerline down each.

2 Start with the buckle end. I used a 5 mm stitch line and a 7 spi (3.85 mm) iron. Normally, when stitching in a loose keep, there would be five holes to keep the buckle in place, then a gap for the keep, and then twelve holes to stitch the keep in. The gap for the keep is equivalent to about five holes; so in total, twenty-two holes would give us the same dimensions as the stitching of a loose keep belt.

In turn, this gives us a stitch line of just over 75 mm; let's call it twenty holes—75 mm of stitching, more than enough.

I have rounded the template I am going to use for my buckle template at one end and added 75 mm of stitching, twenty holes to either side of the card. Counting the holes is better than working to a measurement, since it is more consistent—but try both and see what works better for you.

1

2

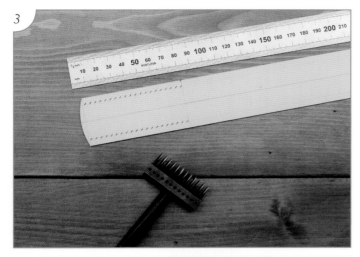

3

4

5

3 Where the stitching ends—or at the 75 mm mark—draw a vertical line across the template: this is not only where the stitching ends but where the slot for the buckle tine starts.

4 I used a 38 mm crew punch to make the slot. With the slot made, add a further vertical line where the slot ends: this is where the face stitching begins.

5 Working from the second vertical line, add a further 75 mm of stitching, or twenty holes. This is the buckle template done. On the surface, it looks fairly simple—and in truth, perhaps it is. The complex bit comes in adding the keep, but that comes later; for now your template should look like this.

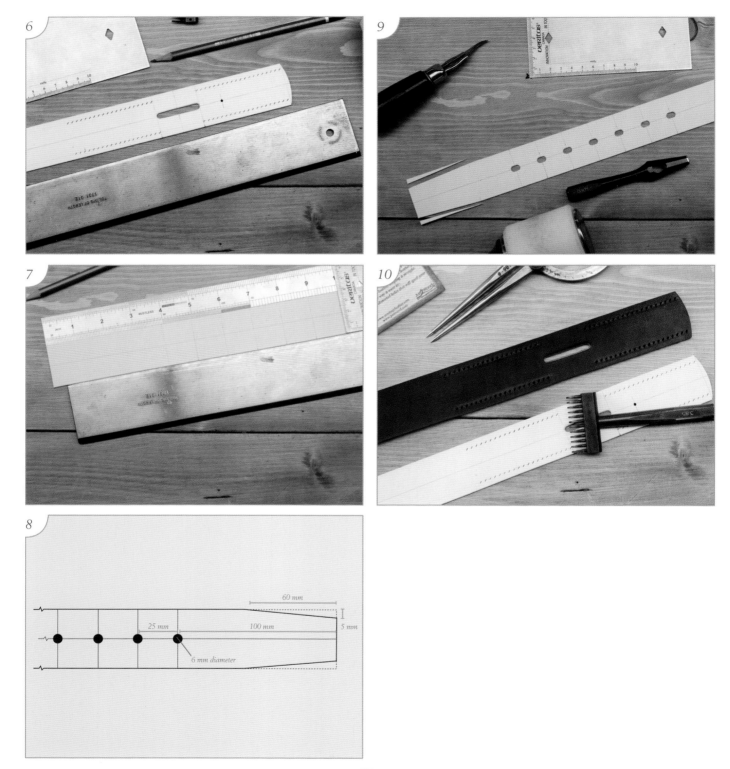

6

7

8

9

10

60 mm

25 mm   100 mm

5 mm

6 mm diameter

6 Finally, add the all-important measuring point. The distance between the two lines at either end of the slot should be 38 mm. Often this can creep up to 40 mm, since the grind of the slot can make the hole bigger. Either way, measure this distance between the lines, divide by two, and add a vertical line directly in the center of the slot.

Now measure the distance on the buckle from the heel bar to the roller bar. My measurement is 38 mm, but yours may differ, so check this. Add this measurement to your buckle template to give your first measuring point.

7 Move on to the billet template. The measurements we have been working with stay the same. The first hole is 100 mm from the tip, with seven holes 25 mm apart. For this belt I'm adding a tapered tip. Using the other piece of 400 × 38 mm card, mark the first hole 100 mm from one end, and then six more holes 25 mm apart.

8 Creating a tapered tip is simple: you just need to work out how deep into the strap you want to cut and how narrow you want the tip to be. In this case, there will be a 28 mm tip. To do this, I marked in from the end of the strap 60 mm, and 5 mm from the edge on either side. You can change these figures to produce whatever style of tip you like.

9 Once you have decided on your tip, transfer all the information over to your template and you are good to go. Make the holes, trim the tapers, and gently round the corners at the tip just to finish it off. On completion, your template should look like the one in the photograph.

10 The keep doesn't really need a template—it is, after all, a simple strip of leather folded around two thicknesses of the belt, dressed, and stitched into place. I cover this in more detail in a moment. Place the buckle template over one end of the leather and transfer all the marks through.

11 With the buckle end marked and ready for its buckle, we need to measure the strap.

Lay the strap out flat on the bench, next to a long ruler or tape measure, with the buckle template laid over the top. Move the ruler so the end or 0 point is sitting in line with the measuring point.

11

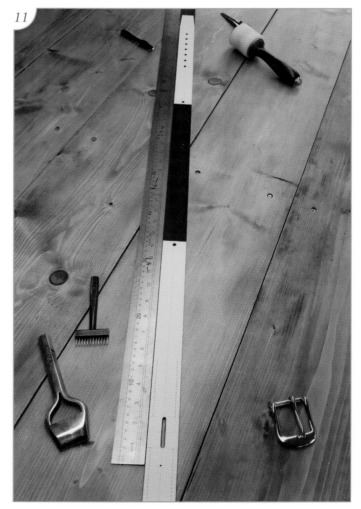

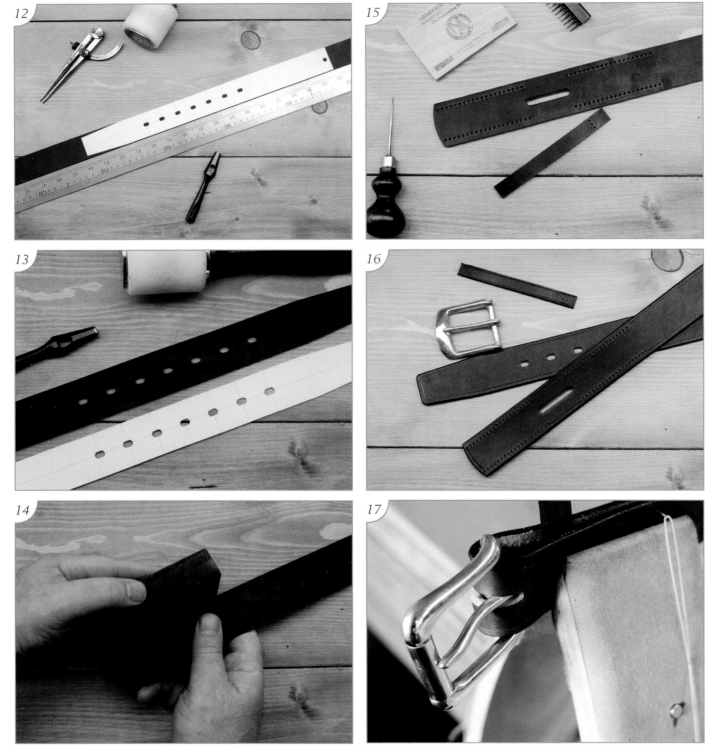

12 Now place the billet template onto the strap so the center hole corresponds to the desired measurement; in my case, I want 965 mm.

13 Transfer all the holes from the template to the leather, along with the lines ready to cut to taper the tip. You can now cut the strap to length and make all the holes and trim the tapers.

14 Lightly sand the points on the edge of the strap where the taper starts as this takes off any sharp edges and rounds the strap nicely into the taper.

15 With the strap cut to length, you should have a sufficient length left to cut a 12.5 mm strip of leather for your keep. This needs to be at least 110 mm long. I am splitting mine from 4 mm down to 3 mm and skiving the ends so they are less bulky as they sit between the front and back.

Bend it around two thicknesses of the belt and cut it so it meets in the middle. Mark on the keep where the stitching will sit, and add three holes for it so it can be stitched into place.

16 With the strap cut to length, all the holes marked and made, and the keep cut to length, it's time to dress them. This is a personal choice—dress your strap and keep in whatever style you want. I shall be adding a crease, beveling the edges, dying them with Edge Kote, and burnishing with wax.

17 It's now time to begin to put it all together. With a stitched-in keep, we have a little more flexibility and can have the keep a little closer to the buckle if we want—or farther away for that matter. If you are using a stiff leather, be cautious of taking it too close, as the tip will be difficult to bend over such a short distance. I'm going to stay close to the measurements we started and catch my keep in the fifth hole from the buckle.

18

18 With one side of the keep held in place, we are ready to stitch the first side. Start stitching from the belt side of the stitch line, stitching toward the buckle.

19 Stitch all the way to the second-to-last hole. Don't forget the locking stitch (as explained on p. 29). At the last hole, pass both needles through it in toward the middle of the belt.

20 Having brought both needles to the middle, put them together and pass them through to the other side, behind the buckle, ensuring you don't accidentally pass them through the loop of the tine.
  Turn the belt over in the clam and set yourself up to stitch the other side. Once comfortable, twist the threads together about twenty times, so they twist tightly. You want the twist to begin to sit up above the edge of the leather when you relax the thread.

21 With the threads nicely twisted inside the belt, behind the buckle, take one needle and pass it through the first hole from inside to out on the front, then the same with the other needle on the back. It does not matter at this time which needle is which.

19

20

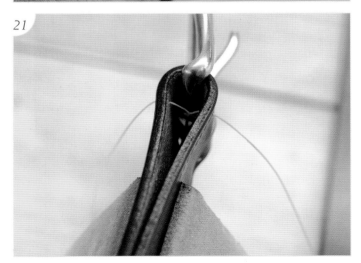

21

22 Now continue stitching as normal, remembering to catch the keep on the fifth stitch to ensure it doesn't sit twisted. Finish the line of stitching as you would normally, and your belt is done.

I'm sure by now you can see that pre-pricking all the holes has made this type of belt so much simpler and, indeed, neater.

Feel free to admire your handiwork!

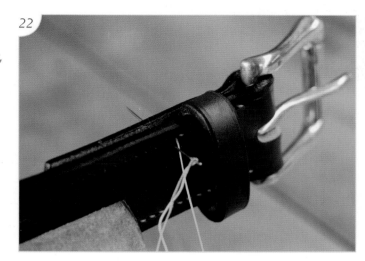

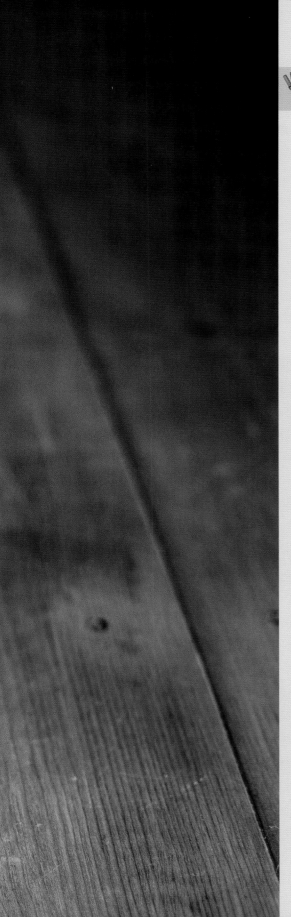

 # SHORT STRAP BELT

As a stand-alone design, there is more work in making a belt in this style. It can be done if you're looking to make something a little more different, but it is an excellent technique to add to your skill set for repairing damaged belts or making a belt out of a strap that would be otherwise too short. It is worth making at least one just to familiarize yourself with the process.

TOOLS & MATERIALS

6 mm hole punches	Pencil	**Body leather:** Black bridle butt
Beveler	Ruler	**Buckle leather:** Aussie nut bridle butt
Card	Ruler stop	**Buckle:** Westend roller brass and steel
Crease	Scratch awl	**Thread:** Tiger, black 0.6 mm
Crew punch (oblong or bag punch)	Skiving knife	
Cutting edge	Slicker	
Disk	Stitching clam	
Dividers	Stitching irons	
Hammer or maul	Strap end punch	
Knife		

PROBLEM-SOLVING

How many times have you gone to make a belt only to find the strap is just that bit too short? Or worse still, you've cut your strap to length, then gone and made a critical mistake. Aaagh! (a)

If you are adjusting or repairing a belt and do not have enough leather in the strap to make the adjustment in one go, this technique of adding a second piece will help keep the original look of the belt. It's a very good trick to get you out of a jam, and I have used it a number of times over the years. It will not fix every problem—and will not give you much more length—but it may just give you enough to get you out of a bind.

Normally, we bend or fold the leather back around the buckle making the return, which is then stitched. On average, it takes up about 125 mm of leather, and this can make all the difference. It is also a brilliant technique for repairing or adjusting an old belt where the leather around the buckle has failed or for a belt that is just a little too short. (b)

Many people will shorten a belt from the billet end; this is not a great idea since it brings the holes too close to the tip of the belt. (inset)

Any of these seem familiar? Adjusting the buckle end can be daunting, which is why adjusting the billet is so tempting—but the technique shown in this belt provides a better alternative. However, with all the possibilities this design of belt offers to get us out of a jam, it's easy to forget it also looks good. It can be made just for the sake of it. It is, after all, different and unique, and furthermore, using a contrasting leather can take your belt a step further.

1 As always, start with the templates needed to make this belt. The buckle template in this instance will be a little different, while the billet template should begin to be familiar. It does, after all, have the same job to do on all belts, so it's going to be quite similar.

The buckle template is a stand-alone piece on this belt, so the template will reflect this. Start with two strips of card, both 38 mm wide, with the short one being 216 mm long and the long one 400 mm. Draw a centerline on each.

2 Starting with the buckle template, cut this to 216 mm. At the center, 108 mm from either end, add a vertical line; this will be at the middle of the slot. I have cut both ends of the template to an English point; you can adjust this to different designs.

From the vertical centerline, mark two further lines 19 mm to either side. These are your outer measurements for the slot and where your stitching starts and finishes. Mark the stitching by starting at the tip and working back to the lines; it is okay if they stop a little short.

1

2

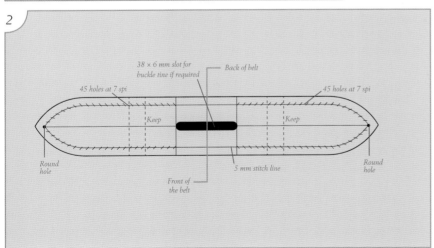

38 × 6 mm slot for
buckle tine if required — Back of belt

45 holes at 7 spi — 45 holes at 7 spi

Keep — Keep

Round
hole — Round
hole

5 mm stitch line

Front of
the belt

3 Now make a start on the billet end. This bit is going to get repetitive, but I'll try to mix the designs up a little to keep it interesting and give you more options.

For now, I am going to stick with the English point, since it will match the plate. If you change the design of the plate, remember to change the tip to match.

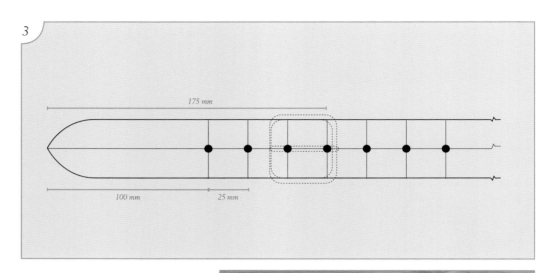

4 One of the most important measurements is the point between the tip and the first hole. It needs to be long enough that should the wearer need to use the last hole, the tip will still be held by the keep. I go into more detail on this subject on **page 26**.

For now, 100 mm is plenty for this task. Add the point, mark the first hole at 100 mm from the tip and six further marks 25 mm apart, and make your holes.

The holes for this belt will be round. I have selected a hole punch that will sit comfortably over my tine; in this case 6 mm (*inset*).

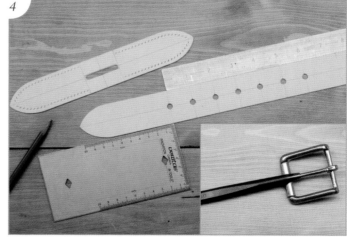

5 With both of the templates made, it's almost time to take them to our leather.

The one issue we haven't yet covered is how to measure the strap or, indeed, where it sits in the buckle plate. One of the better places to stop the strap is in front of the keep—this will give the greatest length advantage to the buckle plate.

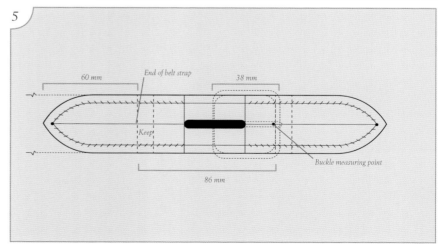

6 In the illustration for step 5, we begin to see how the belt strap will fit into place, and that only 60 mm of the strap is taken up in the process. The buckle I'm using is 38 mm from the heel to where the tine meets the bar. I have, therefore, added a mark to my template at 38 mm; check the measurement of your buckle and add this to your template in the same way.

7 We have to know how long the strap needs to be to make our belt. With the belt in two parts, this gets difficult. An easy way is to measure from the measuring point on the template to the outer edge of the keep, where the strap will sit. On mine, this measurement is 86 mm; so, if I needed a 965 mm belt, I need only measure to 879 mm on my strap.

8 Now place the billet template onto the end of the strap. I have a long ruler for this job, but a tape measure will do just as well. Place the ruler so 0 sits against the end of the strap, then slide the billet template along the strap until the center hole corresponds to 879 mm or the measurement you require.

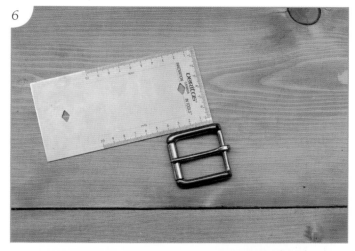

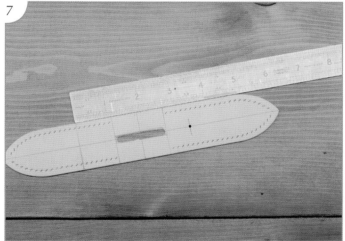

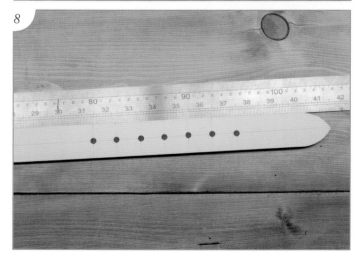

9 With the correct measurement achieved, mark all the holes at the billet end and cut the English point; your strap is now cut to the correct length.

10 The keep on this belt is 12.5 mm wide. I bent it around two thicknesses of the belt and cut it so it meets in the middle. I then marked on the keep where the stitching will sit, so I can add three holes for it to be stitched into place.

11 Using the billet template, mark the holes on the strap where it will be stitched inside the buckle plate. Remember, this is only 60 mm, so don't add too many holes. Next, cut the buckle plate to match the template exactly. Mark and make all the holes for stitching, along with the slot. Dress all of the edges to the desired finish. (I cover this on pages 23–24.) On this belt I beveled, creased, dyed the edge, and burnished.

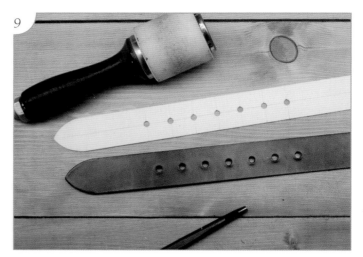

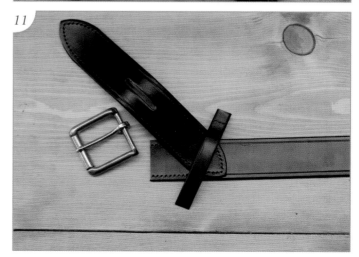

12 Normally, when we make a belt, there are only two layers to consider; with this belt however, we have three layers.

One way to lessen this much bulk is to skive the back of each end of the buckle section where the strap joins it, and then the end of the strap itself. The overlap is 60 mm, so only 60 mm needs to be skived off each part. Tapering the ends makes the transition flow much better, removing bulk but maintaining strength. As a profile view, it looks a little like the diagram. I used my splitting machine to achieve this, but if you look at p. 24 on splitting, I go into more detail and highlight other options if you don't have a splitting machine.

With the ends of the straps skived down, it's time for the stitching. This is simple enough: just one continuous row down toward the point and back; I'm going to take the leap that by this point you have a grasp of the stitching, and leave you to it.

Once stitched, your belt is done!

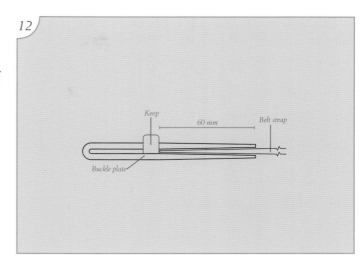

LINED BELT

Lining a belt is definitely taking belt making up a level. It is seen as a mark of luxury, but it can also have other purposes. We may need to hide the rough back of a piece of leather, but given the quality of some of the leathers available today, this is less likely than it once was. Then there's strength—adding a lining is an excellent way to reinforce a belt you want to use to carry heavy items, especially if a reinforcement strip is sandwiched between the two layers. And, finally, grip is one of the more valid reasons for lining a belt.

TOOLS & MATERIALS

6 mm hole punch	Pencil	**Leather:** *Sedgwick's Light Havana*
Beveler	Ruler	**Lining:** *Lamport dark brown*
Card	Ruler stop	**Buckle:** *1½ in. swelled Westend roller*
Creaser	Scratch awl	**Thread:** *Tiger, yellow 0.6 mm*
Crew punch	Skiving knife	
Cutting edge	Slicker	
Disk	Stitching clam	
Dividers	Stitching irons	
Hammer or maul	Strap cutter	
Knife	Strap end punch	

In the past, belts were lined to make the back intentionally rough. For instance, if you had an item you needed to carry on your belt that when reached for was exactly where you left it—such as a knife, sword, or firearm—a way had to be found to ensure it did not slip along the belt, so you didn't waste valuable time hunting for it.

A way of achieving this was to line the belt with an intentionally rough leather such as suede, then adding a matching piece to the inside of the belt loop of the sheath, scabbard, or holster, so that when the item was placed onto the belt and the belt was worn, the rough leathers locked together, preventing items from sliding out of position. For a modern material, Velcro is an ideal choice, but suede is still a very effective alternative.

Friction or reinforcement does not need to be our only reasons, though; sometimes it's just a really nice way to finish a belt.

1 This belt is going to be very similar in design to the Plain Belt with a Stitched Keep (p. 73). Many of the principles will be touched on, but in less detail. If you have already made that belt, much will be clear, but if not, familiarize yourself with that project first.

As usual, start with the templates. This is very similar to what we have already made, but on this occasion, the stitching will continue once we move into the body of the

1

belt. Start with two strips of 1.5 mm stiff card, 38 mm wide and 400 mm long. Add a centerline to each.

2 Buckle template: I have started, as usual, from the right-hand side of the template by adding a gentle curve to make the back look nice. Following a 5 mm stitch line, I added twenty holes at 7 spi (3.85 mm). I used a 5 mm stitch line because the leather is going to be a little thicker and the wider line will suit the belt better.

I then added my 38 mm slot for the buckle and continued the stitching. On this belt the stitching will continue for the length of the belt, with only the first twenty holes securing the back. I have added my measuring point to suit the buckle I'm going to use; in this case, 38 mm.

3 Moving on to the billet end, I am going to stick with seven holes and use an English point. This is a good choice of tip for this belt, since it can help with the stitching. I'll cover this in more detail later on. Using the second piece of card, lay out the holes 25 mm apart and 100 mm from the tip. Hole 4 is the center hole for measuring.

4 With the two templates made, we are ready to take them to the leather. Cut two strips of leather, one for the belt and one for the lining.

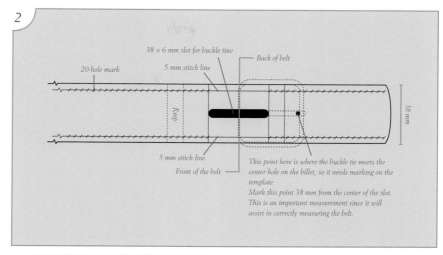

2

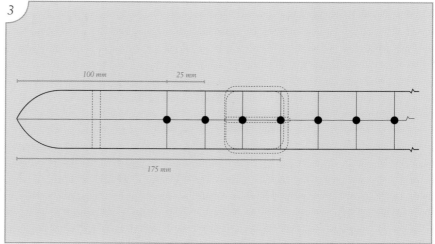

3

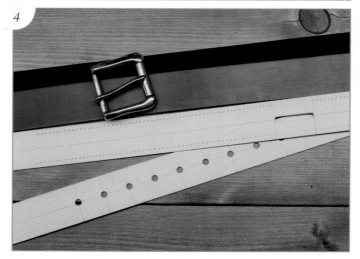

4

5 Start by making holes at the buckle end. Mark out the twenty holes on the return, and only the first two holes of the two lines on the front. Do this lightly, since their position may change. Add the slot and trim the end.

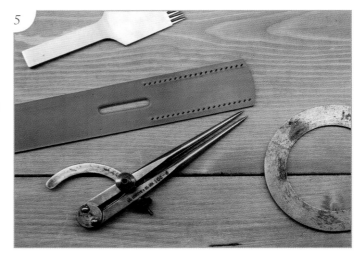

6 Now line up the strap with a ruler on the bench so the 0 of the ruler is on the buckle end measuring point, and the center hole of the billet end lines up with the measurement you want—mine is 840 mm.

7 Mark your holes and where to trim the tip. Then make the holes and cut to length.
   You will notice that we have not covered the stitching on the main body of the belt yet; we need to deal with the lining first.

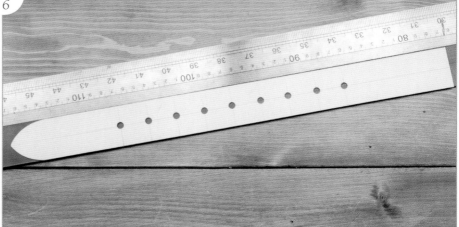

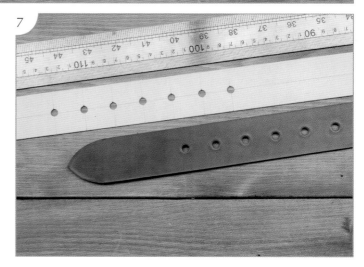

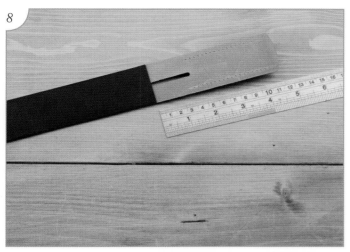

8 The length of belt you require will dictate the length of lining you need. We can save a little in the length of the lining, since it stops at the belt side of the slot. The lining does not need to go all the way to the end of the return, and it can save you 114 mm. This means it gets caught nicely under the return, holding it securely and finishing it off neatly.

9 I used shoulder as my lining. This is firm leather, so I have cut a 38 mm wide strip to length. I'm going to rough up the back of the leather and use contact glue to bond the lining to the belt. The lining needs to be laid over the piece so it drops into place. If you pull the lining too hard and apply too much tension, it can stretch. This is to be avoided since it can distort the belt.

10 Once the lining is on the leather, do not slide your hands along it; this can cause ridges to appear. Instead, press down firmly all along the strap in stages—lifting, moving, and pressing to create the best bond. The edges are the most important, so these can be hammered down.

11 Once the lining has been glued into place and it has had a chance to cure a little, the lining can be trimmed. While it is glued in place, the leather is still soft and flexible, so it needs to be cut very carefully.

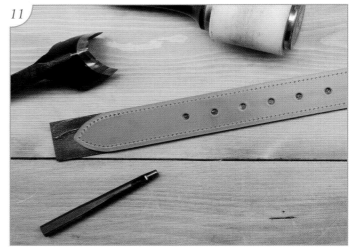

12 On to the stitching. If we had begun marking the stitching where the first hole started at the buckle end, there would be no guarantee that we will get it to fit by the time we get to the tip. This may have given us a long or short stitch that would be a very poor show on a belt such as this. To avoid this, we are going to start marking our holes from the tip and working back toward the buckle end, finishing at the two marks we started with.

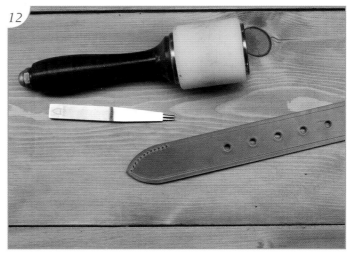

13 If the stitching is going to be out, it is only going to be out by half a stitch from that mark at the most. If this were a stitch, it would be obvious—but if we can lose this in the actual hole placement, it will never be seen, since it is only 2 mm maximum. In the photograph we can see it does not quite meet, so a long stitch has been avoided and the variation will never be noticed. Normally, when making this style of belt, I would not even make the marks.

14 With all of the holes marked on the belt, it's time to consider the design. I want to add a further level of detail with some fancy stitching. I cover this on page 31. I have created a simple design that will be placed at the central point on the belt, between the measuring point and the center hole.

15 Cut the keep before stitching the belt. I used a piece of leather 12.5 mm wide and split down from 4 to 3 mm.
Wrap the keep around two layers of the belt and trim so they meet in the middle. Mark where the stitch line sits, and add three holes for stitching. Skive the ends of the keep down a little to remove bulk, and your keep is done.

13

14
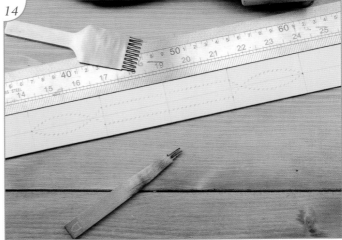

15

16 Dressing the edges. If you have used a firm leather for the lining, beveling the lining in order to dress the edges will not be an issue. If, however, you have used something softer, this may well be difficult and will need more care. The better the bond at the edges, the easier this will be.

17 Stitching the belt in one go will require an awful lot of thread. This is where the English point comes into its own. We can stitch from the tip to the buckle, stitching the belt in two sections; three with the fancy stitching. This makes the stitching a little more manageable. Start with the latter.

18 Starting at the tip, stitch one side of the belt toward the buckle. Don't forget to catch the keep as you go. I have set my keep four holes in from the buckle—holes 5, 6, and 7 hold the keep—so as I stitch toward the end, the first hole that will catch the keep will be hole 7.

Stitch the other side the same and you have a completed belt.

Your belt is now ready to last you several lifetimes. I hope you enjoyed this project and are ready to start the next.

RAISED BELT

This is certainly a belt to challenge the skills and patience, and one to work up to. You don't see too many well-made raised belts because of the time and skill needed to make them.

If you are looking to sell them, the cost runs high, but it's definitely well worth making just for the skill set.

TOOLS & MATERIALS

38 mm crew punch
6 mm hole punch
Beveler
Card
Contact glue
Crease
Cutting edge
Disk
Dividers
Hammer or maul
Knife

Pencil
Ruler
Ruler stop
Scratch awl
Skiving knife
Slicker
Stitching clam
Stitching irons
Strap cutter
Strap end punch

Leather: Lamport dark green
Lining: Sedgwick plain butt Windsor Oak
Buckle: 1½ in. Bristol copper
Keep: 1½ in. flat cast copper
Thread: Amy Roke purplish red 0.55 mm

A raised belt is a stylish thing of beauty when made well, but it's not all about looks. Adding a bolster to a belt is a very good way of increasing its strength if it has a job to do.

If you are of a mind to carry something on your belt, this design is a good choice.

We are going to be using leather for this bolster, but nylon reinforcement strips or even Kevlar webbing can be used if you need a real workhorse.

In its simplest form, the belt is constructed of three parts: the body, which is the part that needs to be strongest; the bolster, which is slightly narrower than the belt and is what gives the belt its raised look and extra strength; and the thinnest part of the whole construction, the overlay. This latter piece is stretched over the bolster, glued, and then stitched into place on the body. A separate lining can be added if desired, but I have a burgundy butt that I am going to have on the inside as my lining.

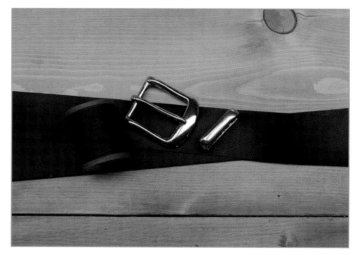

All of these parts can be separate pieces of leather, but if you have a splitter, they can also be cut from the same strap. Using separate pieces is a great way to make a belt if you want to use as the overlay a more colorful or exotic leather that would otherwise not normally lend itself well to belt making. It is also easier since the strap does not require splitting.

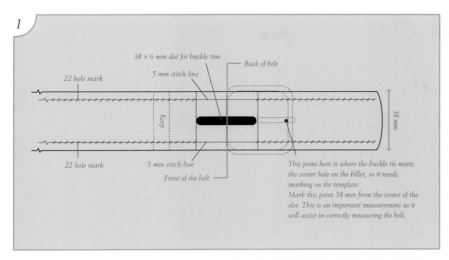

1

22 hole mark

38 × 6 mm slot for buckle tine

5 mm stitch line

Back of belt

Keep

38 mm

22 hole mark

5 mm stitch line

Front of the belt

This point here is where the buckle tie meets
the center hole on the billet, so it needs
marking on the template.
Mark this point 38 mm from the center of the
slot. This is an important measurement as it
will assist in correctly measuring the belt.

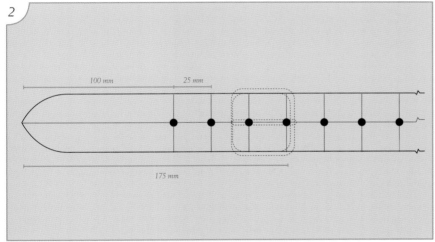

2

100 mm

25 mm

175 mm

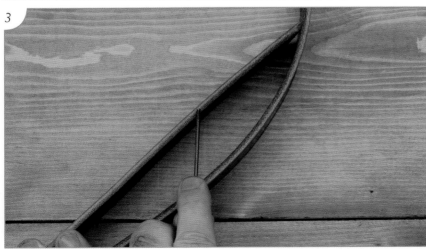

3

1 This style of belt follows on nicely from the Plain Belt and Short Strap Belt projects. It is a natural progression from those belts that helps with building familiarity and consistency. The templates we are using are the same as those in the Lined Belt on p. 91. The buckle template has had a curve added to the back and had twenty holes added following a 5 mm stitch line.

2 Moving onto the billet end, I'm going to stick with seven holes and use an English point. This is a good choice of tip for this belt, as it can help with the stitching. I'll cover this in more detail later on.

Using the second piece of card, lay out the holes 25 mm apart and 100 mm from the tip. Hole 4 will be our center hole for measuring.

3 Strength is always important when making a belt, so using the best leather is a good idea. However, even the best leather is organic, and the thickness can differ from end to end. The thicker part tends to be toward the tail, with the thinner part toward the neck.

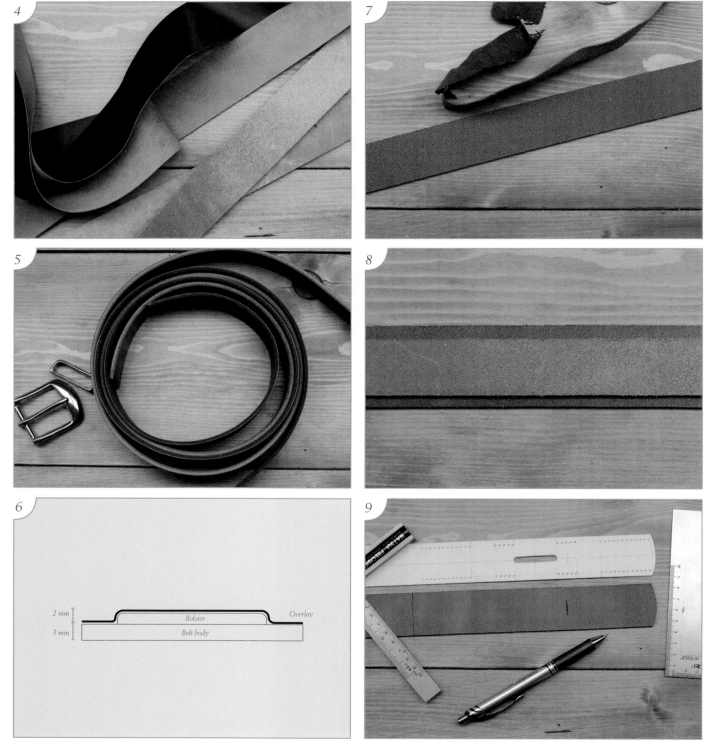

4

5

6

| | 2 mm | | Bolster | Overlay |
| 3 mm | | Belt body | |

7

8

9

4 A more colorful or textured leather for the overlay may be what you are looking for—I've chosen a deep, rich green for mine. This is shoulder and thin, so evidently a poor choice of leather for strength. However, because I am using bridle butt for the body and bolster, this is not an issue and will not affect the belt's strength at all.

5 For this belt, I am using 4 mm bridle for the body, with the back split away to even the strap up. This will then be turned so the top grain of the leather becomes the lining. The overlay will be a piece of shoulder split down to 1 mm thick, and the bolster will be another piece of bridle split down to 2 mm.

6 The biggest issue we face in making this belt is getting the overlay to fit over the bolster and still meet the edges of the belt. The overlay has an extra 4 mm of distance to travel as it goes up, over, and down the other side of the bolster. Not all leathers can accommodate that much stretch, so we must cut our overlay bigger.

We need a piece at least 42 mm wide for it to fit, but to make things a little easier, I'll round this up to 45 mm to give me plenty of room if I vary slightly during the gluing.

7 Having cut the strap and knowing I'll be using the top grain as the lining, I need to even the strap up. Starting at the thin end, I'm going to split the strap, taking the back off. I split the strap facedown, so that means any unevenness to the strap will appear above the blade in the offcut. This will give me an even thickness throughout the strap.

8 I now have two belt components, the core and the overlay. Now I need the bolster.

I've chosen a piece of 2 mm bridle for this, but the material or thickness can vary, making the belt thicker and stronger if you wish. This bolster needs to be narrower than the belt: my stitch line is going to be 5 mm from the edge of the leather, and a further 1 mm needs to be added to allow for the stitching. So, the bolster needs to be set 6 mm in from the edge on both sides, giving a total width of just over 26 mm. The belt will be stitched in the corner where the bolster meets the core. Note that *nothing* at this time is cut to length.

9 The two parts of the belt that will run for the full length are the core and the overlay; the bolster will stop short. Starting with the core, lay the buckle-end template over the top, and mark where the bolster will stop; also mark the measuring point.

10 Line up the 0 of the ruler to the measuring point marked on the leather, and set the billet template on the other end, lining up the center hole with your desired measurement.

10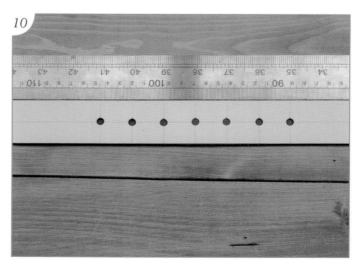

11 Cut the billet end to length.

12 Now to glue the bolster into place. First, if you have cut an English point onto your strap, the same needs to be done to the bolster. It needs to follow the existing cut but 6 mm smaller, since it is forming concentric circles.

For example, if you used a 100 mm disk to cut the English point on the strap, you will need an 88 mm disk to cut the point to the bolster. This keeps the 6 mm difference to ensure our stitching remains consistently placed between the edge of the leather and the bolster. If this varies, it can affect how the stitching looks, although there is a little leeway.

13 With the tip of the bolster cut to match the tip of the belt, place it onto the belt and mark the bolster the same way as you marked the body, so it can be cut to length. Once cut, skive the end to feather it down over about 25 mm to nothing. This will prevent the belt from catching the bolster when it is put through the keep, and remove bulk from the buckle area.

14 The bolster can now be glued to the body. To assist with this, set your dividers to 6 mm and run a line around the body, showing where the bolster will sit. It needs to be centered; otherwise the stitching will be put out of line.

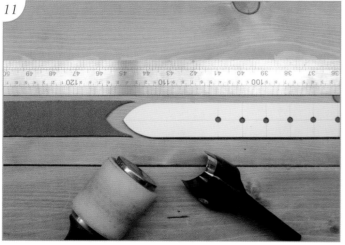

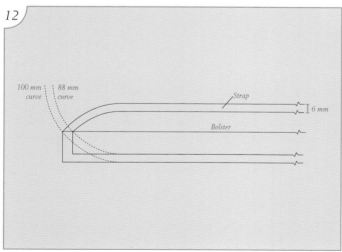

15 With the strap cut to length and the bolster glued into place, it's time to glue the overlay to cover the full length of the belt. Because the overlay is wider than the body, it will be easier to lay the overlay facedown on the bench and take the belt to it. You will have a better chance of keeping everything central this way.

16 Apply gentle pressure to the center of the body, just to get the leather to stick.

Once attached, carefully turn everything over. Now begin to apply pressure to the overlay where it sits over the bolster, but don't get too close to the edges yet.

Don't be tempted to slide your hands up and down the leather, since this can create a bow wave effect and rucks in the leather. Keep the pressure firm, even, and downward, working your way up the full length of the strap to include the buckle end.

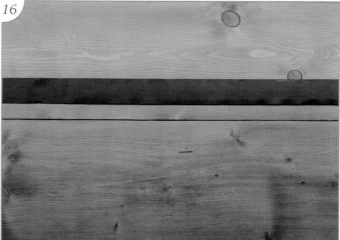

17 With the overlay attached to the bolster, begin to work out toward the edges. With your fingers, find the edges of the bolster through the overlay, and press until they show through. Note that we are still not quite pressing the overlay down as far as to the body yet; we are just beginning to bend the leather around the bolster.

18 Once a nice clear outline of the bolster is showing through the overlay, begin working around the edges with a bone folder, finding the sharp edge to follow with the stitching.

19 Once this is done, it should be looking somewhat like a belt; we just need to trim off the excess overlay.

20 With the overlay trimmed, put the buckle template over the top, mark, and make all of the holes.

21 Do the same for the holes on the billet end.

22 Take the opportunity to give the edges a sanding if needed, and add a bevel and dress the edges. I used Edge Kote and beeswax to do mine. Do this to the entire belt and add a crease to the buckle area and curved end if desired.

My strap is 1.4 m long and will require 760 stitches; this means I need a thread length of about 7 m. I can halve this by stitching to and from the tip. If you are able to stitch both left- and right-handed, you can stitch from the tip toward the buckle twice. This will halve your thread, bringing each run down to 3.5 m, which means having threads no longer than 1.75 m per side. This is not a job for linen, but certainly achievable.

Your belt may be a different size to mine, so take a look at the thread length calculator on p. 33 to see what you may have to manage.

Stitch your belt and you are done; you have a raised or bolstered, lined belt.

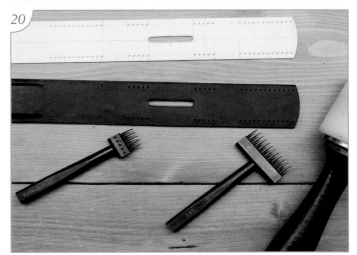

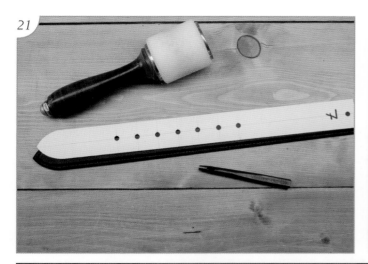

HOBBLE BELT

The hobble belt, or at least the process of hobbling animals, has been round for some time—there are ancient Egyptian hieroglyphs depicting the process, and many cultures have one version or another.

Possibly one of the most famous types is the Australian stockman's belt, also called the hobble belt. Two rings or squares were added to make it a three-part belt, thus allowing the billet to be fed through both rings to make a figure-eight restraint, which was used around the front legs of a horse. The horse still had mobility, albeit limited, but could be found in the vicinity in the morning. When not in use as a hobble, it could be worn as a belt.

How practical it would be for you today is for you to decide! The rings certainly make ideal locations to attach hooks or tethers to, and it is also a nice talking point to have in the workshop. Another nice touch is that you can add a sheath or pouch to accommodate a small tool or knife on the leather between the two rings.

TOOLS & MATERIALS

38 mm crew punch

6 mm hole punch

Beveler

Card

Contact glue

Crease

Cutting edge

Disk

Dividers

Hammer or maul

Knife

Pencil

Ruler

Rule stop

Scratch awl

Skiving knife

Slicker

Stitching clam

Stitching irons

Strap cutter

Strap end punch

Leather: Sedgwick plain butt Windsor oak

Buckle: 1½ in. Westend steel

Rings: 1½ in. cast square

Thread: Tiger, black 0.6 mm

1 The billet end and how the buckle is attached are very similar to that of the Plain Belt with a Stitched Keep (p. 73), with just the addition of the two rectangles. This means that three parts are required for the belt instead of one: four with the keep.

2 The parts of the belt are broken down into three sections: the buckle section, the bridge, and the billet. These sections are joined, in my case, by metal rectangles that are 42 mm wide and 56 mm high and are made from 7 mm bar. Alternatively, rings also work well.

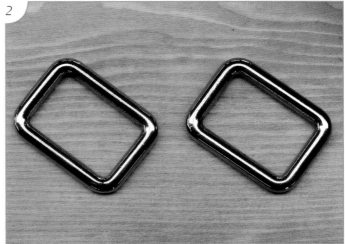

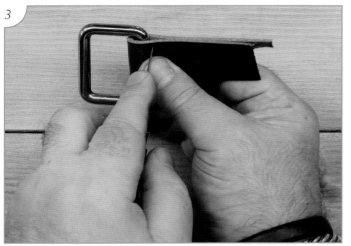

3 To calculate how much leather I will need to attach to the rectangles, I have taken a piece of the leather I'm going to use and wrapped it around one of the bars. Then I mark where my stitching will sit on the front and the back—the marks are 36 mm apart. This, with the width of the rectangle, will give me an idea of how much space they take up.

4 A thinner or thicker leather will change this measurement, so check this calculation against the leather you're using.

Start with the templates. I have three strips of 1.5 mm thick, stiff card, 400 mm long and 38 mm wide, and have run a centerline down each. Start with the buckle end.

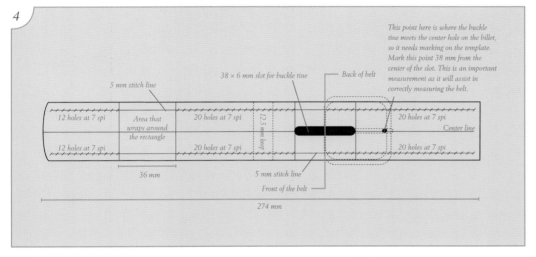

This point here is where the buckle tine meets the center hole on the billet, so it needs marking on the template. Mark this point 38 mm from the center of the slot. This is an important measurement as it will assist in correctly measuring the belt.

38 × 6 mm slot for buckle tine — Back of belt

5 mm stitch line

| 12 holes at 7 spi | Area that wraps around the rectangle | 20 holes at 7 spi | | | 20 holes at 7 spi |
| 12 holes at 7 spi | | 20 holes at 7 spi | *12.5 mm keep* | | 20 holes at 7 spi |

Center line

36 mm   5 mm stitch line

Front of the belt

274 mm

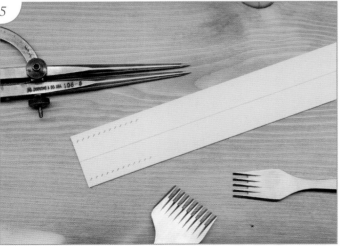

5 I used a 5 mm stitch line and a 7 spi (3.85 mm) iron. This is a stitched-in keep belt, so twenty holes will be used—this gives us 75 mm of stitching. I have left the end of the template straight, since this will be tucked under the return that holds the rectangle at the other end, and the first set of holes will be placed one stitch from the end.

6 Where the stitching ends, or at the 75 mm mark, draw a vertical line across the template, to mark where the slot for the buckle tine starts.

7 As usual, I used a 38 mm crew punch to make the slot. With the slot made, I added a further vertical line where the slot ends; this will be where the face stitching begins.

8 Working from the second vertical line, add a further 75 mm of stitching, or twenty holes.

9 Now for the all-important measuring point. The distance between the two lines at either end of the slot should be 38 mm, and half of this is 19 mm. The distance from the heel bar to the roller is 38 mm, so mark 38 mm toward the return from the slot centerline.

10 With the stitching for the buckle done, let's look at where the first rectangle wants to sit. It needs to be about 100 mm away from the buckle. With the length of the buckle and stitching that I have, this has worked out about right.

I know I will need a 36 mm gap to stitch my first rectangle in place, so I have added a line where my twenty-hole stitching stops, and measured another line 36 mm from there and then added twelve holes. Then I curved the end of the template. This will match all the returns on both of the rectangles.

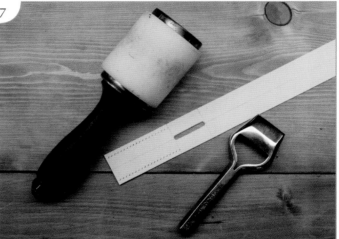

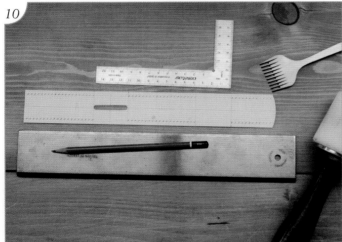

11 The bridge is the section of leather between the two rectangles and sets the distance between the loops. If you want the loops closer or farther apart, this is the piece you need to adjust.

The rectangles are the same size, so the 36 mm gap between the stitching needs to be maintained. I kept my hole count to twelve and the distance between the rectangles at 150 mm. The last hole of the stitching sits about 6 mm away from the rectangle, so the gap between my two outer holes wants to be no more than 138 mm.

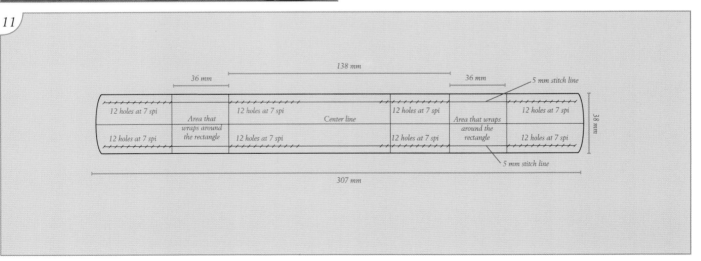

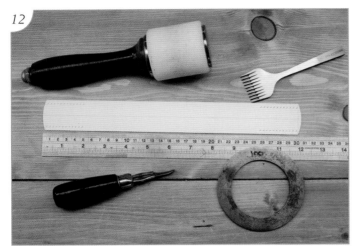

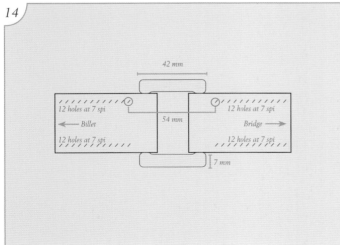

12 Here we can work to a specific measurement: I cut my template to 307 mm and rounded both ends with a 100 mm disk. I then added twelve holes to each end.

13 At the end of the stitching, I added two lines 36 mm apart to highlight the fold around the rectangle. Inside the second set of lines, I added twelve more holes. I did the same to both ends, meaning that the outer two holes of the face stitching will be 138 mm apart, or close—close will do absolutely fine.

14 Now for the billet template: this is the longest piece of the belt but has two worked ends. Normally this would mean another template, but we can be clever here. We need to find a fixed point on each template to help us get the correct overall measurement for the belt; this can be the last hole of our stitch lines on the rectangles circled below.

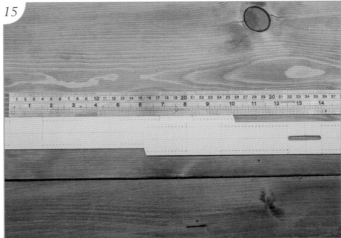

15 The distance between these two points is 54 mm. On the buckle template, the distance from the measuring point to the corresponding hole is 130 mm; between the two corresponding holes on the bridge section, the measurement is 138 mm.

Adding all of these together:
130 mm (buckle) + 54 mm (first rectangle) + 138 mm (bridge) + 54 mm (second rectangle)

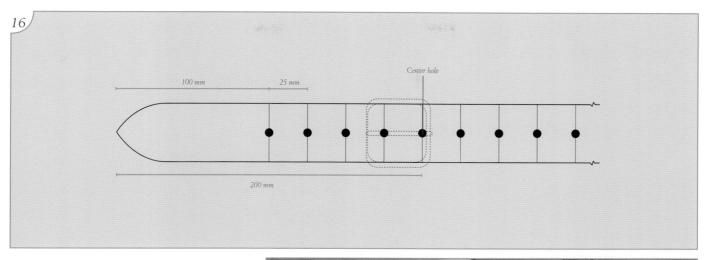

This gives us an overall measurement of around 376 mm, and is a fixed measurement. As long as we don't change anything on the buckle or bridge parts, this will always be that length.

So, if we want a 965 mm belt, we only need to measure 594 mm along the strap from the center hole, to mark where the last hole on the stitch line needs to sit to get the length of strap we need.

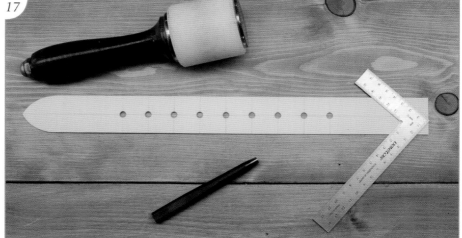

16 In view of this, we can move forward with the billet template. I have chosen nine holes to give a greater range with the loops.

17 As before, choose your tip, mark 100 mm to the first hole, and mark a further eight holes at 25 mm increments.

18 Now all the templates are made, and with a good idea of how to measure, cut a long strip of your chosen leather. I used a strip of 4 mm (13 oz.) thick bridle butt that is about 1.6m long, so more than long enough for my three pieces, plus a bit left over for my keep. Starting with the buckle end, place the template over the top of the thin end of the strap. Mark and make all of the indicated holes and cut to length.

19 Repeat the process with the bridge template, marking and making all of your holes, then cut to length.

20 Moving ont o the billet end, leave the strap as long as possible and place the billet template over the top of the thick end. Cut the tip, mark, and make all the holes.

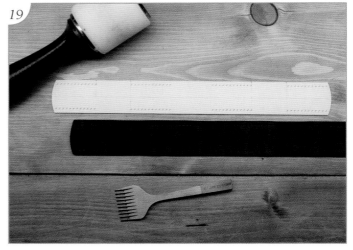

21 Cutting the billet to length is not as complicated as it may sound. We know the measurement from the measuring point (A) to the end hole of our stitching (B) on the second rectangle—376 mm.

22 We just take 376 mm off our final measurement. I want a belt of 965 mm, so removing 376 mm leaves me with 589 mm. I now measure 376 mm from my center hole and make a mark on the leather where my last stitch hole (B) will sit.

23 I can now take the bridge template and, using the right side, line up the B hole with the mark I have just made on the leather, then make all the holes and cut the strap to length.

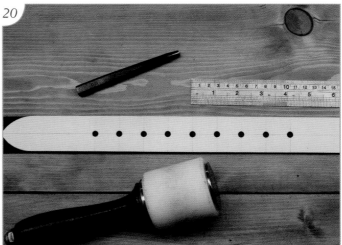

21

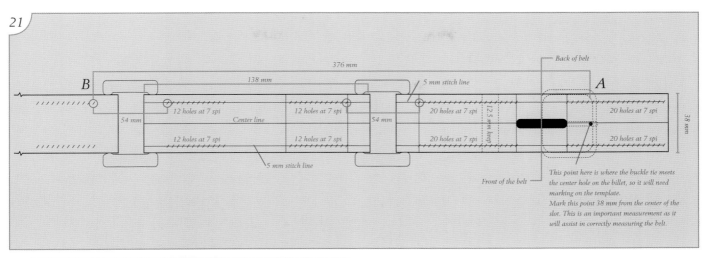

376 mm

138 mm

B

5 mm stitch line

Back of belt

A

54 mm

12 holes at 7 spi

Center line

12 holes at 7 spi

54 mm

20 holes at 7 spi

12.5 mm keep

20 holes at 7 spi

38 mm

12 holes at 7 spi

12 holes at 7 spi

20 holes at 7 spi

20 holes at 7 spi

5 mm stitch line

Front of the belt

This point here is where the buckle tie meets the center hole on the billet, so it will need marking on the template.
Mark this point 38 mm from the center of the slot. This is an important measurement as it will assist in correctly measuring the belt.

22

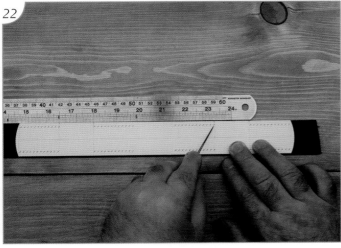

23

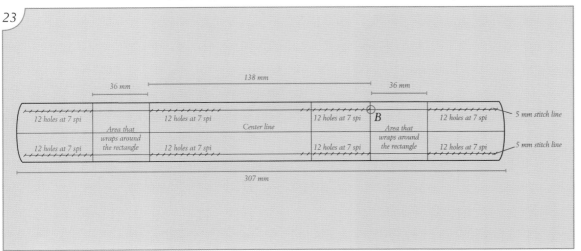

138 mm

36 mm

36 mm

12 holes at 7 spi

Center line

12 holes at 7 spi

B

12 holes at 7 spi

5 mm stitch line

12 holes at 7 spi

Area that wraps around the rectangle

12 holes at 7 spi

12 holes at 7 spi

Area that wraps around the rectangle

12 holes at 7 spi

5 mm stitch line

307 mm

24 Now for the keep. Cut a strip of leather 12.5 mm wide. It needs to be at least 105 mm long. I split mine down from 4 to 3 mm and skived the ends so they are less bulky as they sit between the front and back.

Double-layer two strips of the belt and wrap the keep around, making sure it meets in the middle. Be a little generous with this, since you do not want it to be too tight. Mark where the stitching will sit on the keep with a scratch awl.

25 We are stitching at 7 spi (3.85 mm), which means the keep will have three holes and be caught by four stitches, making it very strong. Add the three holes to the stitch lines you have marked, centering the holes.

26 All the straps are cut, holes made, and ends trimmed. Add any creases you want, bevel, Edge Kote, and finally burnish. This is also a good time to add your maker's mark if you have one.

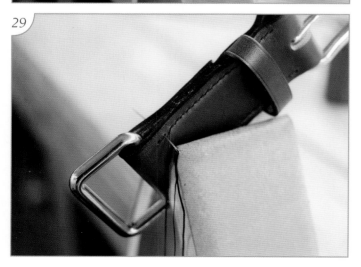

27 One final thing to do is to skive all the returns down before stitching. This does not need to be much—just enough to reduce the bulk a little—and certainly by no more than half the thickness of the strap.

28 Stitching the buckle and keep into place will be done together with the first rectangle, since it is caught by the same rows of stitching. The curved return for the rectangle needs to sit on top. Using a couple of needles to line up your holes, put the buckle in place, with the keep trapped between the front and the return. I am setting my keep four holes in from the buckle. Trap the first rectangle between the front and the return at the other end, and place it all into the clam.

29 Starting at the rectangle end, add the backstitches. I used three and stitched down toward the buckle, catching the keep on the way. Once you have stitched one side of the belt, put your needles through, turn it over, and stitch the other side, remembering to catch the keep four holes from the end on the way.

30 Once you have finished that row of stitching, add one end of the bridge section.

Stitch everything the same by starting with three backstitches. Pass the needles through to the other side and finish with three backstitches.

31 Stitch in the second rectangle to the other side of the bridge as before; nothing changes.

32 Finally, stitch the billet to the second rectangle to finish off the belt. It is at this point we can take the completed belt to the ruler to make sure everything has worked out and that the center hole is indeed where it needs to be.

You're done! I'm sure you will now appreciate that adding rings, squares, or rectangles to a belt can be a bit of a pain, and that you have to have a good grasp of measuring. This is precisely why the Hobble Belt is toward the back of this book! It does not look that complicated, but it is easy to get lost. Enjoy your belt in whatever manner you see fit.

30

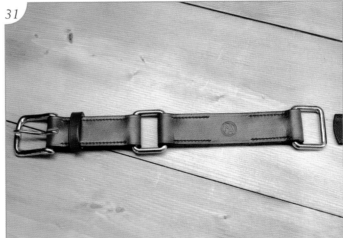

31

32

BUSHCRAFT BELT

This is a utility belt with a reinforced recess and pinch plate. I think this belt is a good step back toward the true origins of the belt and its original purpose—a device to help carry and keep close our most precious personal things.

In times past, this would likely have been flint and steel, a knife, tinder, and food. The belt kept these items at hand and secured them with loops and pouches. This remained the case right up to the invention of pockets.

Today, the modern backwoodsman or bushcrafter follows much the same principles: if it's secure, it can't be dropped or lost. A good, well-made belt will ensure that pouches, sheaths, holsters, and tethers remain exactly where you left them—on your belt!

TOOLS & MATERIALS

38 mm crew punch
6 mm hole punch
Beveler
Card
Contact glue
Crease
Cutting edge
Disk
Dividers
Hammer or maul
Knife

Pencil
Ruler
Ruler stop
Scratch awl
Skiving knife
Slicker
Stitching clam
Stitching irons
Strap cutter
Strap end punch

Leather: *Oak bark bridle butt in dark stain*
Buckle: *2 in. two-prong Westend roller brass*
Thread: *Tiger, black 0.6 mm*

Here's my list of requirements for a belt of this style that suits how I want to use it. Yours will probably differ, so create your own list of requirements to make the belt fit your individual purpose better. This is one of those pieces of equipment where the adage "If you fail to plan, you plan to fail" fits well. We are looking at all the points where a belt can fail, and factoring them out.

This belt is more likely to be exposed to the elements, so you will need a good-quality leather designed to be used outdoors. I am using bridle butt.

It may well carry heavy or multiple items, so it has to be robust. My leather will be 5 mm thick and 50 mm wide. If you have a thinner leather, you can always line it to bring the strength up. (*a*)

It has to be secure, with no risk of coming off on its own. I am using a double-prong solid-brass buckle (*inset*), stitched into place and reinforced.

It may need to be worn over light clothing as well as foul- weather gear, so it needs to be adjustable. I am adding two rows of fifteen holes—this also helps fit it to other purposes should the situation dictate. I designate hole 8 as my center hole. (*b*)

a
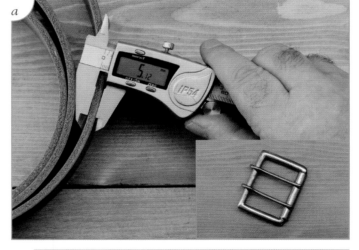

b

The extra holes will mean a longer billet, especially in summer clothing, so it will have a stitched-in keep and a running keep. (*c*)

This belt will be used to carry a knife on a regular basis, so it will be reinforced and have a recessed area to stop the sheath from sliding. (*d*)

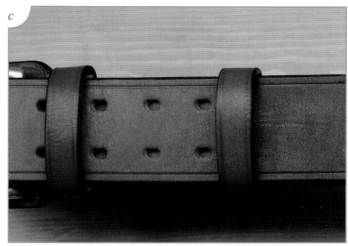

c

d

1 As usual, start with the templates. First, check the internal measurement of your buckle. Mine is 50 mm, so I'll cut my templates to 50 mm wide and 600 mm long. Although both the prongs sit off-center, still add a centerline, since this will help with some additional stitching. Having the prongs evenly distributed across the width of the belt looks much smarter. I have set mine in 14 mm from the edge and added lines to both templates accordingly.

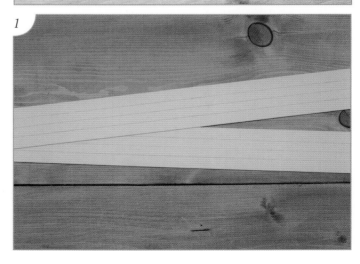

1

2 As we have done before, round the end of the strap to ensure it fits nicely against the body. For this I used a 125 mm disk.

3 Add a 5 mm stitch line to either side of the template. Marking in from the curve one full stitch, add twenty holes to each side. I used a 7 spi (3.85 mm) iron to do so. Once you have added your holes, draw a vertical line across the template, marking the point where the stitching stops and the slots start.

4 Normally, the length of the slot is dictated by the width of the belt, because this allows for the prong to run freely in the slot. Usually, as the buckle gets bigger, so does the prong—and so in turn does the slot. That would mean the slots on this belt would need to be 50 mm long. However, this belt has two prongs that are the same size as those found on a 38 mm buckle. In view of this, 38 mm slots will work nicely. Take care when placing the slots. The 14 mm lines act as guides that run through the center of the slots.

I have measured the width of my crew punch, and it is 6 mm wide. So, where my slots will sit, I can add two further lines from each side of my guidelines, one at 11 mm and the other at 17 mm. Each is exactly the same length as the crew punch, and this gives me a frame in which I can place the tool to ensure it is straight.

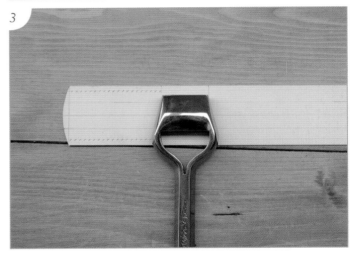

5 Punch both slots into your template. When done, add a further vertical line to mark where the slots end and the stitching starts. While doing this, mark the center of the slots between these two lines, so the buckle measurement can be added later on.

Now to add the holes; in this case, twenty-one of them. This places one stitch over the end of the return, locking it down. The belt is wider than normal, so this will help a lot.

6 The belt now needs a further set of holes, a lovely point of reinforcement. Starting at the return side of the template and following the centerline, add twenty-one holes—this will take your stitching to within one stitch of the end of the leather. Moving to the other side of the slots, add a further set of holes to the centerline, but on this occasion, add twenty-two holes to accommodate the over stitch.

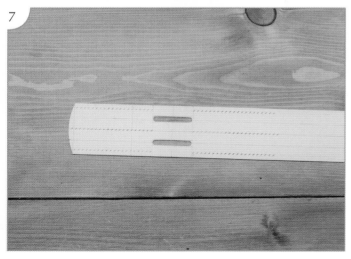

7 One further measurement needed is the length of the buckle. Mine is 38 mm, bizarrely enough. Mark clearly from the centerline in the middle of the slots ,out toward the return, to make the measuring point.

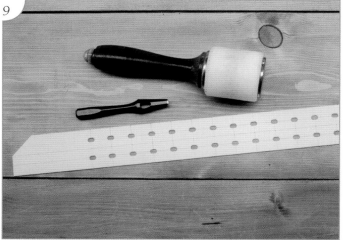

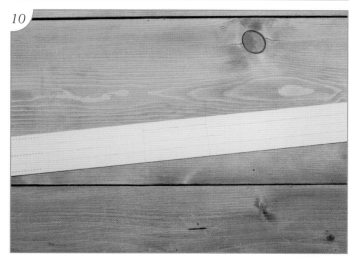

8 We've not quite finished with the buckle template yet, but set it aside for the moment. Now to begin working on the billet template. Make sure you have the two 14 mm lines in place, and choose whichever tip you prefer for this belt. I am going for a clipped corner. This is quite simple: mark 25 mm in from the end and 25 mm from the bottom, and cut a corner off at 45 degrees. The corners can be rounded to soften the look.

9 From the end, mark a line at 100 mm: this will ensure there is enough leather at the end of the billet to be caught by the keep if you have to use the last hole. This is also the position where the first hole will sit. From this point, add your desired number of holes; I am adding fifteen to each side. A belt of this style is extremely versatile and can be used for many purposes in many ways, so you cannot overdo the hole count!

10 This next stage is totally optional and can be skipped if you do not want a recess.

I would use a belt of this sort for carrying a camp knife, but with moving round, bending over, and lots of sitting, the knife can move around the belt. I discussed the benefits of a lined belt and a patch inside the belt loop in the Lined Belt on page 91. Here, we are going to look at another way of keeping something in place.

Take the knife you would carry in camp, put it on a belt, and wear it in the position you want it to sit. Now, measure from the front edge of the sheath to the hole on the buckle you are using, and the width of the loop on the sheath. For me, these measurements are 290 mm, and just over 80 mm. I am left-handed and the billet will face left, so I add these measurements to the buckle template.

11 If you are right-handed and have the billet facing left, add this measurement to the billet template, using hole 8 as your center hole (if you are following the same principles as I am).

12 The recess is just a shallow indent into the leather, no more than 10 mm deep and, in my case, 80 mm long. The corners have been rounded to soften the harsh edges, and a plate will be stitched over the top to reinforce this area. The idea is to prevent the leather folding at this point with use over time. Camp knives can be heavier, so a bit of reinforcement can't hurt. If you carry a much lighter knife, you may not need the recess.

13 Now look at the reinforcement template. The plate we are going to stitch over the top will be the same size as the belt, with the two ends cut to reflect the belt tip.
You can make this as simple or elaborate as you wish. The piece I need for this will be 130 mm wide and 50 mm high. I'll add the recess to the center top—exactly as the belt—and round the corners slightly.

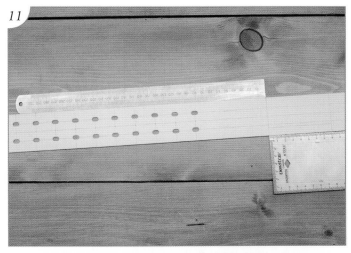

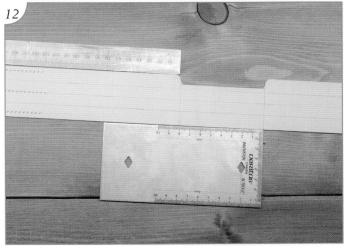

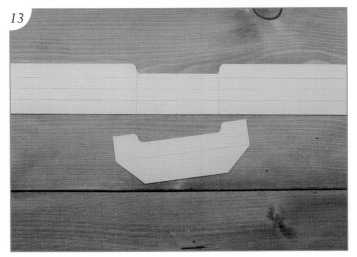

14 With a belt of this style, one that will predominantly be worn over clothing, a pinch plate is an excellent addition to prevent clothing trapping in the buckle when doing it up. It is a simple-enough design based on two rectangles, one for the belt and one for the buckle.

I know the size of my belt: my buckle is just over 52 by 67 mm. The rectangle for the belt wants to be 100 mm wide by 50 mm. I want to add a 4 mm lip on the top and bottom, and an 8 mm lip at the front of the buckle section—which means I will need a rectangle 60 mm wide by 75 mm high for the area of the buckle.

15 Now to add my stitch holes: twenty for the outer edges and twenty-one for the center. This will sit on the back, so it needs to match the back exactly. After that, it can be trimmed to size and rounded to match. I'm also going to round the front two corners where the buckle sits, and curve into the belt from the outer edge from the back, so the whole thing should look like the illustration.

16 With the templates taken care of, take them to the leather. Having cut a strip of 5 mm (13 oz.) thick leather 50 mm wide, I start by adding the curve, all of my slots, and then stitch marks.

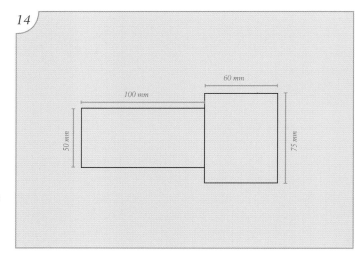

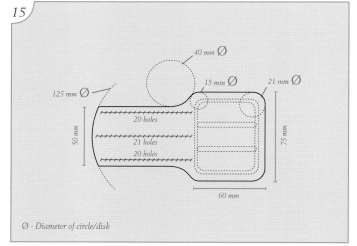

Ø - Diameter of circle/disk

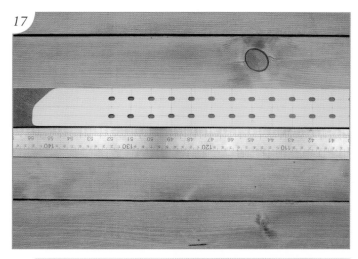

17 Lay the strap out straight, overlay the buckle template, and set a long ruler next to the strap. Set the 0 next to the measuring point and set the billet template on the other end, lined up with hole 8 (the center hole) against the measurement to suit you. My starting measurement is 965 mm—the same as a normal belt. Since this belt may well be worn over the top of another and not as tightly, I have added a further 50 mm, so now have a working measurement of 1.15 m.

18 Cut the strap to length, clip the corner, and make all the holes. I am also rounding the corners slightly to soften them. This is your opportunity to apply whichever tip to the belt you desire.

19 If you haven't already, cut some strips of leather for two keeps. I am having mine at 17 mm wide, which fits nicely between six holes and has four holes in each end, meaning it is caught by five stitches and is very, very, strong!

Wrap one of the keeps around two thicknesses of the bent to mark the center and where your holes will sit. Be a little generous; you may be putting this belt on with cold hands one day, and a slightly bigger keep will do the same job just as well.

20 Cut out your pinch plate and reinforcement piece if you are having the belt loop recess, and dress all of your edges. I will be adding a crease and beveling, and blacking up the edges with Edge Kote and beeswax.

21 Just prior to stitching the belt together, I skive the return down. I can bring this quite thin toward the tip, since the pinch plate will be sitting over it. Equally, I can do the same to the pinch plate, since this will help lessen the bulk.

22 Time to stitch the buckle end, which can be done in three separate rows for ease.

You will not be able to pass the needles through to the middle row of stitching, and passing it all the way to the other side is a little too far.

23 If you haven't already—and you are having one—stitch the reinforcement plate into position. This is a fairly simple process that can be done either by pre-pricking the holes or gluing it into place, then punching through as one.

The final thing to do is to stitch your running keep; I have overlapped mine by ten holes and am running a stitch line down both sides.

You now have a very robust belt, fit for almost any situation. All that is left is to put the phone on silent and hit the wilderness.

20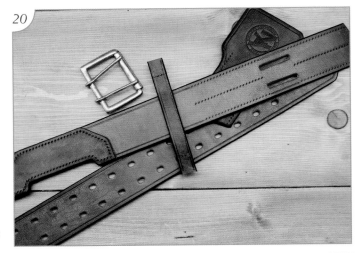

21

22

23

SAM BROWNE BELT

If there was a belt to epitomize the phrase "Necessity is the mother of invention," this belt fits the bill. The concept was born to the mind of General Sir Sam Browne, who, after losing his left arm in 1858, needed to find a way to support the scabbard while drawing his sword, a job usually done by his now-absent left hand. The design caught on and is now part of the uniform for all commissioned officers in the British army, as well as being found in use by various regiments and police forces across the globe.

Originally, the belt was passed through the two-prong buckle, with the billet being held in place by both a keep and a stud. The buckle is actually rather narrow, and for this to be effective, the leather has to be quite light and flexible, 3 mm (7–8 oz.) maximum. Today, this has become a very popular stand-alone belt design used without the shoulder strap, frog hook, or rings, and it's ideal for carrying heavy or multiple items. That and it just looks good!

TOOLS & MATERIALS

38 mm crew punch	Pencil	**Leather:** *Aussie nut bridle butt*
6 mm hole punch	Pippin punch	**Buckle:** *Sam Browne 2 in. brass*
Beveler	Ruler	**Hook:** *Sam Browne 2 in. brass*
Card	Ruler stop	**Thread:** *Slam, beige 0.6 mm*
Contact glue	Scratch awl	
Crease	Skiving knife	
Cutting edge	Slicker	
Disk	Stitching clam	
Dividers	Stitching irons	
Hammer or maul	Strap cutter	
Knife	Strap end punch	

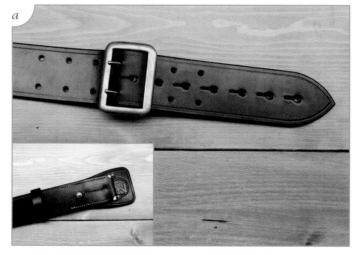

a

A thicker leather is needed to cope with the additional weight, and this alters how the belt is done up. The buckle is too narrow for a heavy 5 mm (13 oz.) leather—it just does not bend well enough over such a short distance for easy and regular use—so a hook system is introduced instead. The way this works is that the buckle is put into position at the billet end. (*a*)

At the back of the buckle is a lower center bar that sits nicely in a pair of hooks on the hook plate. (*inset*)

Once the buckle is hooked in place, a Sam Browne stud pushes through the leather to help hold it in place. A running keep then slides over to lock everything into place. (*b*)

Visually, I am going to keep the belt as close to the original design as possible. There will be less stitching—this is a time thing—but a tapered pinch plate will be added. The buckles come in various sizes, as do the hooks:

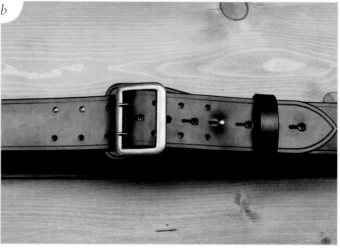

b

a.   38 mm
b.   50 mm
c.   56 mm
d.   63 mm

I am using a 50 mm buckle and hook in brass. One thing you will notice is that the prongs are fixed, so we already have a measurement for these: they are 14 mm in from the edge of the buckle to the center of the prong.

1 For the template. Two pieces of 1.5 mm card, both at 50 mm wide, with a centerline through each. The prongs on my buckle are set 14 mm in from each side, so I'm adding two 14 mm lines from each template edge.

2 The biggest distinction about this belt is that the buckle does not sit at the buckle end; it sits on the billet. So the template normally referred to as the buckle template is now going to be called the hook template, since this is where the hook plate sits. Its construction is simple enough; it just looks complex.

3 I want the leather to sit comfortably around the body of the hook plate, and for that I need my stitching to be 30 mm apart. I did this by bending a piece of the leather I'm going to use for the belt around the body of the hook plate, and marked the leather where it meets the edge of the hook plate on both the front and back.

1

2
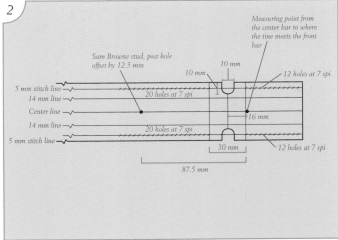

3

4 The first job is to add a 5 mm stitch line to each side of the template, then add twelve holes to secure the return. Following this, draw a vertical line where both rows of stitching stop. Then add a further vertical line 30 mm on for the bend of the leather, or follow your own measurements if yours are different. Divide this measurement by two and draw a vertical line between the two to make a centerline.

5 I'll use twenty holes to attach the pinch plate (see the illustration for step 2), so beyond the second vertical line, add your twenty holes to each side of the template.

6 Now add the indents for the hook plate to sit in. The hooks on my plate are about 10 mm deep, so I will be adding some indents that are 10 mm deep and 20 mm wide. For this I'm going to use a 20 mm wad punch.

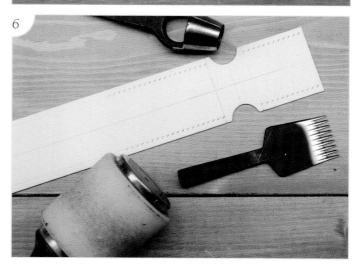

7

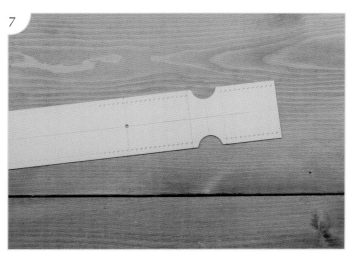

7 The final hole is for the Sam Browne stud. This helps lock the billet down once the buckle has been put in place. We need to avoid too many holes in the same place—there will already be two sets of holes for the buckle, and now we need a third set for the stud.

To make this work better, the stud hole is offset by 12.5 mm to the prong holes, which separates everything nicely. To achieve this, we know that if we mark 100 mm down from the measuring point (where the center hole will sit), a pair of holes on the billet would line up nicely. So, we need to take 12.5 mm off this measurement and mark at 87.5 mm from the measuring point. This will offset the studs by half.

8

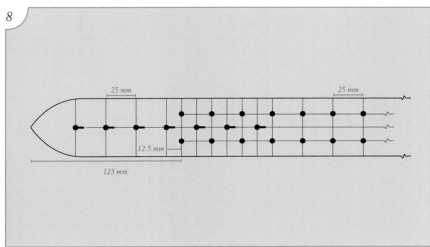

8 Now to look at the billet. We have renamed the other, and while this is now where the buckle will actually sit, I will still refer to it as the billet. First, having added my center and 14 mm lines, I cut an English point—you can choose differently, but it is close to the original, so that's what I've gone with.

9

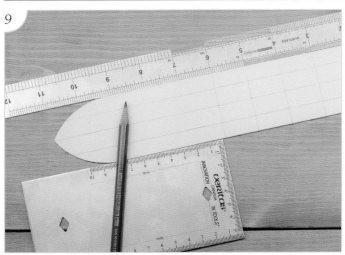

9 As can be seen in the illustration for step 8, there are three rows of holes. We will start with those for the buckle: these are 5 mm holes and are set 25 mm apart. I have chosen to have seven, but you can adjust this if you wish. The first hole is set 125 mm in from the tip. The main reason for this is that the first stud hole needs to be 87.5 mm ahead of this first hole to engage with the stud. So, working from the tip, I have drawn in my first hole line and then six more at 25 mm intervals.

10 Add the line for the first stud hole 87.5 mm ahead of the first hole line. Then a further six at 25 mm intervals, giving a total of seven. This second set of holes is what we have offset to maintain as much strength as possible.

11 Punch all the buckle holes in the template. I used a 5 mm punch for mine—they suit my buckle—but make sure to check yours. Punch all the stud holes. To do this, I used a pippin punch, but a hole punch and slot can also be used. With all the holes and end cut, the template is done.

12 Let's take a look at the pinch plate. The height of my buckle is 64 mm. I have allowed for 2 mm space at the top and bottom, so the widest part of my plate is 68 mm. This then tapers gently down to the width of the belt over the full length of the plate. This means the plate rises early from the belt, giving it the more classic look. I then added 50 mm beyond the stitching for the buckle to sit, and to give the plate a bit of a lip. With the stitching and a 125 mm curve at the back, the plate becomes 130 mm long overall.

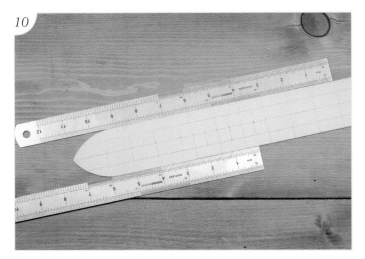

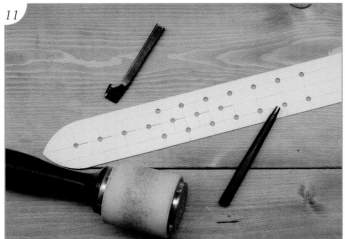

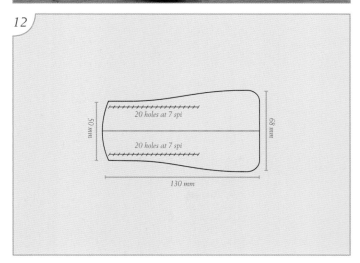

50 mm

68 mm

20 holes at 7 spi

20 holes at 7 spi

130 mm

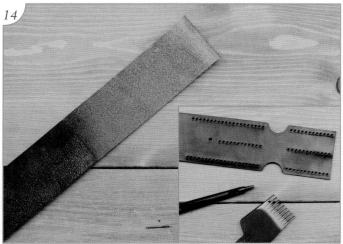

13 The final bit of preparation is for the keep. I have mine at 17 mm wide and 177 mm long. There is only one, and it's a running keep. As we have done before, wrap this around two layers of the belt, overlapping enough for eight holes, and mark the leather. I used a pen.

14 Before working the leather, it needs skiving. Once the indents have been made, this is a little harder, and if you are using a splitting machine, it can go very wrong. Trust me on this—doing it first will avoid any heartache. Skive off the back of the return, from where the slots start to the end. Take no more than 2 mm.

Staying with the hook end, place the template over the strap. Transfer all of your marks through to the leather and make all the stitch holes, the stud hole, and indents (*inset*).

15 With a ruler, measure your belt to the desired length, using the two templates to measure between the measuring point and center hole.

16 Using the billet template, cut your chosen end, mark, and make all of the holes for the buckle and the stud holes.

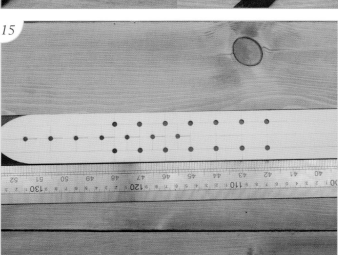

17 Cut the pinch plate to size. I have kept mine quite traditional, even though I used the new closure style. You can play with your own design of pinch plate or, if you intend to wear this as a pants belt, leave it off entirely. I skived the narrow end down for the length of the stitching, again taking off no more than 2 mm.

18 Mark and taper your keep. I tapered mine to 25 mm on the inside of both and added eight holes to each side on both ends, ready for stitching.

19 Add a crease and dress the leather. If ever there was a belt that needed a crease, it's this one.

20 Once the belt is stitched, you will not be able to get to the back of the Sam Browne stud—meaning you need to fit it well the first time! Add a little contact glue (I used Loctite) to the thread and, using a screwdriver, ensure it is nice and firmly placed.

21 Now it's time to stitch the belt together. Catch the hook in the folded leather and add the pinch plate to the back. Line everything up with a couple of needles and place it into your clam.

Stitch as normal for all three rows, and your belt is done. This is the simplest version of a Sam Browne belt, but it can have so much more—fancy stitching, loops, or even lining. The heavy-duty belts even have reinforcement strips inside to stop distortion. These I will let you ponder: for now, enjoy your belt.

17

18

19
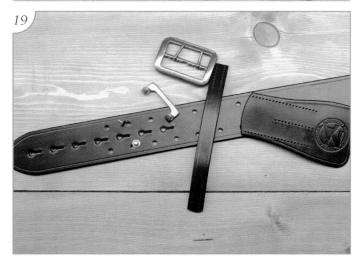

RANGER BELT

In its simplest form, the Ranger Belt is two belts in one, with one stitched over the top of the other. The design was popularized in the United States by the Texas Rangers in the mid-1800s—hence its name today, and theirs remains the most recognized and iconic version of this belt. The design, or at least the idea of the design, could well be much older and may have been used by the Greeks and Romans several thousand years before—and, possibly, even in a galaxy far, far away by the Jedi.

The Ranger Belt bears a striking resemblance to how a girth or cinch is attached to a saddle, and we've been using those since around 700 BCE. Origins aside, the point I'm trying to get across is that it can clearly be seen why this style of belt has been historically favored, and still is today, for being so strong and durable. It is, after all, a double-thickness belt!

I have seen two variations of the belt I'm going to make, the traditional two-part and the more western three-part. The latter is closer to the Texas Ranger version. Sadly, I don't have access to those amazing buckles you see on the originals, and don't tool my leather, so I could not do the western version justice. In view of this, I will make mine a more traditional full-strap, two-part version with a simple brass roller buckle, and use traditional fancy stitching to add detail. I am also simplifying the symmetry and dimensions to make it easier to follow to get the techniques across—but you can defer to whichever design you prefer.

Sizing is an important factor when making this belt. Just taking a measurement from a belt someone is wearing and applying it to a Ranger Belt will not quite work—it'll probably be slightly too small. There is, after all, a whole additional layer of leather now sitting behind it. This makes the distance it travels greater, so the belt needs to be a little larger. Using a thinner leather will negate this, but it can also make the belt weaker.

I am going to refer to the smaller belt that sits on the outside as the "over belt," and the larger one that sits behind as the "body," since this is what carries everything.

TOOLS & MATERIALS

38 mm crew punch
6 mm hole punch
Beveler
Card
Crease
Cutting edge
Disk
Dividers
Hammer or maul
Knife

Pencil
Ruler
Ruler stop
Scratch awl
Skiving knife
Slicker
Stitching clam
Stitching irons
Strap cutter
Strap end punch

Leather: Sedgwick's Light Havana bridle butt
Buckle: 1¼ in. Westend copper
Thread: Amy Roke, beige 0.55 mm

1 Let's just touch on the width of the belt for a moment: this is totally adjustable, and you can work to whichever width you desire. I like to follow the size of the buckle, the narrow strap made to fit in the buckle, and the broader strap suited to the width of the buckle. In this instance I have chosen a Westend buckle from Abbey England, which takes a 32 mm strap.

I'm going to match the width of the body to the width of the buckle. I think this offers a nice symmetry to the belt. It acts as a pinch plate, and the buckle does not extend beyond the leather, so visually it's quite tidy. Of course, you can use any combination you prefer, but the techniques used to make the belt remain the same. In view of this, I am cutting two straps: the first at 32 mm wide and the second at 48 mm (*inset*).

2 This belt will need two keeps, one for the billet of the over belt and one to keep the body in line. This second keep sits on the inside of the belt. In view of this, I will cut two strips of leather 14 mm wide. I cover keeps in detail in the Hobble Belt on p. 111, but I will go into a little more detail here, since one will be reversed.

3 The over belt for all intents and purposes will be very similar to the Lined Belt (p. 91), with the exception that it will only be stitched to the body up to the billet. Note that the billet needs to be kept free.

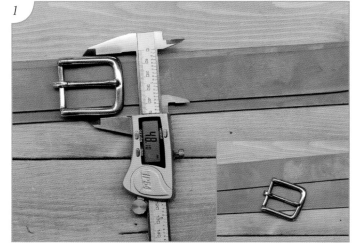

3

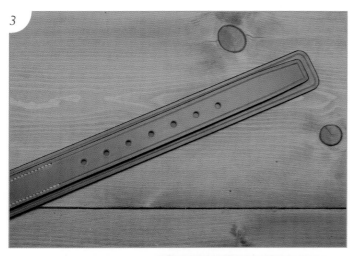

4

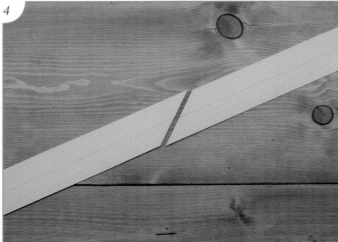

4 First make the templates—three in total for this belt. I cut two strips of 1.5 mm (1,500 micron) thick card to 32 mm wide and 400 mm long, one at 48 mm wide, and added a centerline to each. The wider template will need to be about 1.35 m long, so you may have to join two pieces together. The final measurement will be dictated by the length of belt you are making, so get it as big as possible to start.

5 I hope by now you have a reasonable understanding of making templates. All keeps will be stitched in, so there will be no gaps. Start with twenty holes. The slot length is usually reflected by the belt width, but this buckle has a thick tine, so I need mine to be 38 mm.

I have covered this in other projects so will leave the template below at 32 mm long, in case your buckle tine is slimmer (to give you the choice). The keep for the billet is set four holes down from the slot, with the second keep set immediately behind it.

5

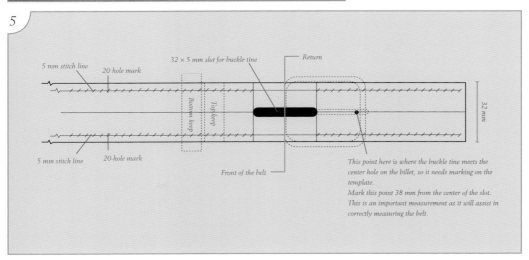

5 mm stitch line   *20 hole mark*   *32 × 5 mm slot for buckle tine*   *Return*

Bottom keep   *Top keep*

32 mm

5 mm stitch line   *20-hole mark*

Front of the belt

This point here is where the buckle tine meets the center hole on the billet, so it needs marking on the template.
Mark this point 38 mm from the center of the slot. This is an important measurement as it will assist in correctly measuring the belt.

6 The billet template changes very little from the other belts we have made. I chose seven holes and a tapered tip for this one. We will discuss where the stitching stops once the template is made and we have it in front of us.

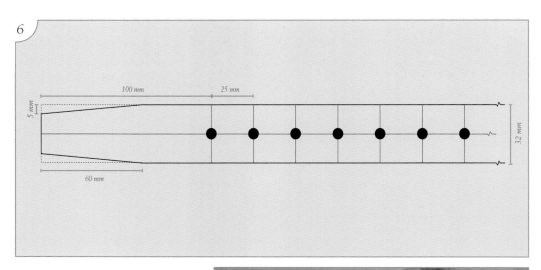

7 In preparation, mark and make all of the holes in your templates as highlighted in the illustration for step 6. My strap is 32 mm wide. Yours may differ, but apart from the width, they should look the same.

8 We haven't yet established where the stitching will stop on the over belt at the billet end—we don't want it too close to the last hole, in case we want to use it. A measurement of 25 mm is about as close as can be managed, but it will be tight—38 mm would be far better. This is close enough to keep the billet straight while still giving enough space to use that last hole.

Note:
I'm going to touch on the sizing of the belt for a moment here, since I make reference to a specific size while measuring the body. If our required measurement is 1.12 m and then we add an extra strip of leather to the inside, our over belt will have farther to travel, and the center hole will be out of line. To accommodate this, add an extra 25 mm to the measurement to get it to fit correctly. The measurement I need is 1.12 m, so I am going to work to 1.14 m.

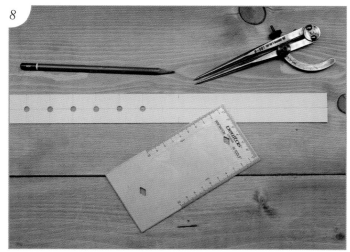

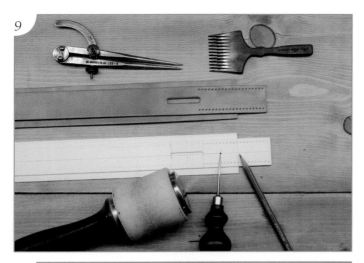

9 The over belt templates are ready, so now pay attention to the body template. It should already be cut to width; in my case, 48 mm—the outer measurement of my buckle. Cutting it to length will be the next task. I want the end of my body to sit slightly proud of the buckle by about 12.5 mm or so. The measuring point on the over belt is inside the buckle, which is about 10 mm thick. To accommodate the width of this and the required extra lip, I am going to add an extra 20 mm to my overall body measurement.

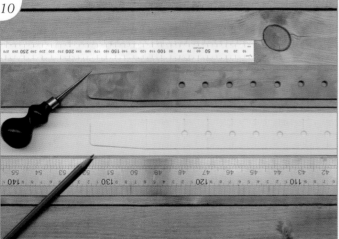

10 If I were to measure along the template 1.16 m from the tip of the buckle, it would sit right under the center hole of the over belt. The body needs to extend beyond this, so that when it's worn it locks together under the second keep. 178 mm will make this fit, taking it almost to the end of the over belt.

11 So, with my belt measurement now being 1.14 m, plus my extra 178 mm for the overlap of the body behind the billet and my additional 19 mm for the lip at the buckle end, I know that my body needs to be 1.34 m long.

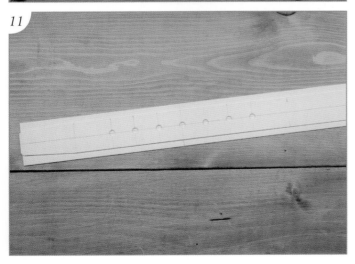

12 The over belt can be stitched to the body in one of two ways. We can either pre-prick all the holes on both parts and stitch without having to glue, or we can glue the over belt to the body and punch through or stitch with an awl. I will pre-prick all the holes in mine first, this makes adding the keeps much easier. To do this, overlay the buckle template over the body template, with the measuring point 20 mm in from the end.

Now to begin to mark through where the holes start. This stitch line is 5 mm in from the edge of the over belt and 10 mm in from the edge of the body. This can be extended with a set of dividers set at 10 mm, with the stitching stopping 38 mm from where the first hole would sit. This will be 200 mm from the end of the body. It wouldn't hurt to count your holes to ensure they match (*inset*).

13 Let's take what we know to the leather. I will need one strap 32 mm wide for the over belt, and another 48 mm wide for the body. Check to see which end of your strap is the thickest; this will be the billet end. At the thinner end, add all the stitch marks and slot. I'm leaving the end straight, as this will be tapered and tucked between the belt and the body.

14 Lay the strap next to a ruler, setting your templates over the top. Move the billet template to the desired measurement—mine is the 1.14 m mark—and cut.

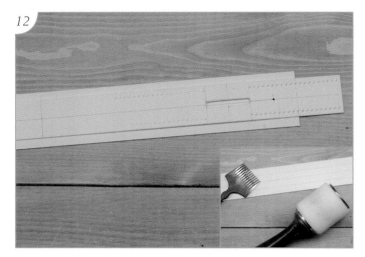

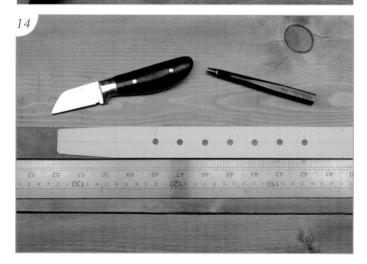

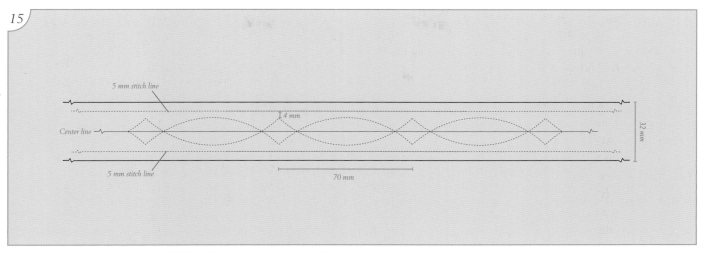

15

5 mm stitch line

14 mm

Center line

5 mm stitch line

32 mm

70 mm

16

17

15 In addition to the 5 mm stitch line to either side of the strap, I am also adding some traditional fancy stitching to the belt. This is a simple equestrian design made by overlapping curves. Look on p. 91 (the Lined Belt) to see how to create this, but here is the design I used.

16 Let's look at the keeps. I have cut mine ready at 14 mm wide. Double-layer the over belt and wrap one of the keeps around and cut to length so they meet in the middle. Then mark where your stitching will sit on the keep with a scratch awl. I am stitching at 7 spi (3.85 mm), which means each keep will have three holes and be caught by four stitches, making them very strong.

17 Repeat this with the body for the reverse keep. Once done, add three holes to each end of each keep, where you marked with the scratch awl. Once you have made your holes, skive the ends down from the holes to the tip on the back of the leather.

18 With both straps and keeps cut to length, and all holes marked and made, we can dress our leather. I am adding a crease to the body, beveling, and Edge Koting all the edges and giving them a good burnish with beeswax.

19 The final task before stitching is to skive down the back of the over belt. Since this is being trapped between the front part of the belt and the body, we can take this quite thin over a long taper—do not take off much from the slot area though! We need to keep the leather strong here, so take just enough to make it bend nicely—no more than 0.5 mm. We don't need to stitch through both layers of leather for the fancy stitching if we don't want to. It is, after all, just decorative. In view of this, the fancy stitching can be done on the over belt first.

20 We're now in a position to stitch the belt together. Bend the over belt to trap the buckle. Using a couple of needles to line the holes up, put the over belt and body together, with both keeps trapped between, the first keep four holes in from the end, and the body keep alongside it. Then place it on your clam. Make sure your keeps are facing the right way, and begin stitching.

21 Once you have stitched one side of the belt, turn it over and stitch the other. I have stitched one side right-handed and then the other left-handed; both can be done either way.

 Due to the length of stitching, both can be done as independent lines.

And you are done! You have made your Ranger, or London lap belt. The first thing you will notice is its absolute strength. This is a perfect belt if you carry something of weight on your belt, and it will last several lifetimes!

18

19
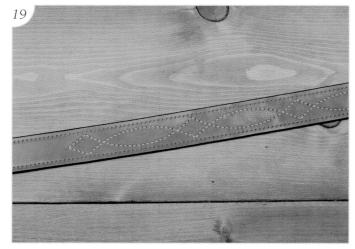

20

21

SUPPLIES

Being in the UK, I'm mainly going to list UK suppliers. However, all those listed do ship internationally, so if you have seen something I have used that you would like to try, you can.

Don't forget to search locally though; you never know what may be nearby.

I shall describe the item and provide the website, you may have to do a short search.

When speaking with the suppliers, tell them I sent you; they may not give you discount, but you never know—I might get some!

Supplier	Item	Size/Type	Website
Abbey England	Saddlers Clam	–	www.abbeyengland.com
	Screw Crease	–	
	Rivet Setter	14g	
	Dividers	6in	
	Crew Punch	1 ½in	
	Bone Folder	8in	
	Strap End Punch	1 ½in (38 mm)	
	Irons	7 spi (3.85 mm)	
Artisans Leather	Strap Cutter	Wood	www.artisanleather.co.uk
Axminster	Rule	Various	www.axminster.co.uk
	Rule Stop	–	
Black Mountains Leather Co	Maul	48 oz Round	www.blackmountainsleather.com
		32 oz Round	
		24 oz Round	
	Beveller	0 & 1	
	French Skive	No6	
Barry King	Crew Punch	48 oz Round	www.barrykingtools.com
		32 oz Round	
		24 oz Round	
		0 & 1	
		No6	
Crafts by Littlebear	Amy Roke Irons	7 spi (3.85 mm)	www.craftsbylittlebear.com
	Amy Roke Thread	0.55 mm Beige	
		0.55 mm Purplish Red	
Crimson Hide	Irons	7 spi French 3.85 mm	www.crimsonhides.com
	Weights	–	
	Sanding Blocks	Large	
	Hammer		
	Leather Rougher		

Supplier	Item	Size/Type	Website
George Barnsley	Plough Gauge	LH	www.georgebarnsleyandsons.co.uk
	Scratch Awl	Clicker	
	Beveller	No2	
	Screw Crease	–	
	Clickers Knife		
H Webber & Sons	Snips	TC1	www.hwebber.co.uk
	Splitter	84	
Horseshoe Brand Tools	Strap End Punch	1 ½in – 1 ¼in	www.ranch2arena.com
	Shoe Hammer	–	
	Dividers	–	
	French Skive	4	
	Beveller	1	
John James	Needles	No 4 Saddlers Harness	www.jjneedles.com
Just Wood	Slicker	Round and Flat	www.justwood.com
	Pulling Block	Various	
KS Blade Punch	Irons	7 spi (3.85 mm)	www.ksbladepunch.com
	Hole Punch's	Various	
Maun	Cutting Edge	Various	www.maunindustries.com
Palosanto	Beveller	1 and 2	www.palosanto-factory.com
	French Skive	12 mm	
Partwell	HY78 Cutting Board	25 mm	www.partwell.com
Terry Knipschield	Knife	Shark	www.leathertools.net
	Skiving Knife		
	Draw Gauge Knife		
Weaver Leather Supply	Draw Gauge Knife	Master Tools	www.weaverleathersupply.com

YEOMAN'S BELT

Item	Description	Supplier	Website
Leather	Printed Dry Butt	Abbey England	*www.abbeyengland.com*
Buckle	2in Centre Bar	Abbey England	*www.abbeyengland.com*
Rivets	Saddlers Rivets	Abbey England	*www.abbeyengland.com*

RIVETED BELT

Item	Description	Supplier	Website
Leather	Black Bridle Butt	Metropolitan Leather	*www.metropolitanleather.com*
Buckle	1 ½in Westend Steel	Abbey England	*www.abbeyengland.com*
Keep	Flat Cast Steel	Abbey England	*www.abbeyengland.com*
Rivets	Tubular Rivet Closed Stem	Abbey England	*www.abbeyengland.com*

MEASURING BELT

Item	Description	Supplier	Website
Leather	Natural Tooling Butt	Metropolitan Leather	*www.metropolitanleather.com*
Buckle	1 ½in Westend Roller Steel	Abbey England	*www.abbeyengland.com*
Thread	Tiger, White 0.6 mm	Abbey England	*www.abbeyengland.com*

PLAIN BELT – LOOSE KEEP

Item	Description	Supplier	Website
Leather	Dark Havana Bridle Butt	Abbey England	*www.abbeyengland.com*
Buckle	1 ½in Bristol Brass	Abbey England	*www.abbeyengland.com*
Thread	Tiger, Black 06 mm	Abbey England	*www.abbeyengland.com*
Keep	Strip Formed Belt Loop	Abbey England	*www.abbeyengland.com*

PLAIN BELT – STITCHED KEEP

Item	Description	Supplier	Website
Leather	Sedgwick Plain Butt Windsor Oak	Abbey England	*www.abbeyengland.com*
Buckle	1 ½in Swelled Westend Roller, Brass	Abbey England	*www.abbeyengland.com*
Thread	Tiger, Yellow 0.6 mm	Abbey England	*www.abbeyengland.com*

SHORT STRAP BELT

Item	Description	Supplier	Website
Body Leather	Black Bridle Butt	Metropolitan Leather	*www.metropolitanleather.com*
Buckle Leather	Aussie Nut Bridle Butt	Metropolitan Leather	*www.metropolitanleather.com*
Buckle	Westend Roller Brass and Steel	Abbey England	*www.abbeyengland.com*
Thread	Tiger, Black 0.6 mm	Abbey England	*www.abbeyengland.com*

LINED BELT

Item	Description	Supplier	Website
Leather	Sedgwick's Light Havana	Abbey England	www.abbeyengland.com
Lining	Lamport Dark Brown	Metropolitan Leather	www.metropolitanleather.com
Buckle	1½" Swelled Westend Roller	Abbey England	www.abbeyengland.com
Thread	Tiger, Yellow 0.6 mm	Abbey England	www.abbeyengland.com

RAISED BELT

Item	Description	Supplier	Website
Leather	Lamport Dark Green	Metropolitan Leather	www.metropolitanleather.com
Lining	Sedgwick Plain Butt Windsor Oak	Abbey England	www.abbeyengland.com
Buckle	1½" Bristol Copper	Abbey England	www.abbeyengland.com
Keep	1½" Flat Cast Copper	Abbey England	www.abbeyengland.com
Thread	Amy Roke Purplish Red 0.55 mm	Crafts by Little Bear	www.craftsbylittlebear.com

HOBBLE BELT

Item	Description	Supplier	Website
Leather	Sedgwick Plain Butt Windsor Oak	Abbey England	www.abbeyengland.com
Buckle	1½" Westend Steel	Abbey England	www.abbeyengland.com
Rings	1½" Cast Square	Abbey England	www.abbeyengland.com
Thread	Tiger, Black 0.6 mm	Abbey England	www.abbeyengland.com

BUSHCRAFT BELTS

Item	Description	Supplier	Website
Leather	Oak Bark Bridle Butt in Dark Stain	J & FJ Barkers	www.jfjbaker.co.uk
Buckle	2" Two Prong Westend Roller Brass	Abbey England	www.abbeyengland.com
Thread	Tiger, Black 0.6 mm	Abbey England	www.abbeyengland.com

SAM BROWNE BELT

Item	Description	Supplier	Website
Leather	Aussie Nut Bridle Butt	Metropolitan Leather	www.metropolitanleather.com
Buckle	Sam Browne 2" Brass	Abbey England	www.abbeyengland.com
Hook	Sam Browne 2" Brass	Abbey England	www.abbeyengland.com
Thread	Slam, Beige 0.6 mm	Stonesfield Leather	https://sfleather.co.uk

RANGER BELT

Item	Description	Supplier	Website
Leather	Sedgwick's Light Havana Bridle Butt	Abbey England	www.abbeyengland.com
Buckle	1¼" West End Copper	Abbey England	www.abbeyengland.com
Thread	Amy Roke, Beige 0.55 mm	Crafts by Little Bear	www.craftsbylittlebear.com

ACKNOWLEDGMENTS

I want to thank Sam, my glamorous assistant and PA, for keeping me sane, feeding me coffee, and proofreading my drivel so I could adjust it and turn it into a book. I even made her learn how to use a camera—that was a laugh!

Jenny, who already works so hard, still found time to come and help me where she could. Jennyboo—it is appreciated.

And Stevie, my daughter. She didn't spend as much time in the workshop as perhaps she would have liked. She was, after all, studying for her master's—so a reasonable-ish excuse. But, we shared writing issues, ideas to deal with word blindness, TikTok clips, and jokes. Dr. Bea, you were more support than you know.

You each get a Ferrari in the color of your choice.

For some amazing photos, I would like to thank Jason Elberts of Jet Productions. They are easy to spot, I am in them, and they look amazing. Thank you, Jason, for making me look good.

Finally, I would like to thank the amazing folks at Abbey England and Metropolitan Leather for providing me with the leather and buckles used to make these belts. As ever, your support is appreciated.

ABOUT THE AUTHOR

"From the moment I fashioned my first item from leather, I was hooked".

I put that in my first book and it still stands true today. I love what I do as much as ever.

I am a full time leatherworker and teacher of those skills. The reward I get from making something is nice, but, the reward I get from teaching someone to do the same is far more valuable and stays with me.

Writing has given me the opportunity to reach more people on yet a different level.

I have enjoyed writing this book because belts are cool, although it could do with being 3 times as thick! I hope your knowledge and enjoyment of leatherwork is increased by what I put into this book.